SNAPP
SHOTS

SNAPP
SHOTS

USING SMARTPHONE APPS FOR INVENTIVE PHOTOGRAPHIC RESULTS

ADAM BRONKHORST

APPLE

First Published in the UK in 2012 by
Apple Press
7 Greenland Street
London NW1 0ND
www.applepress.com

10 9 8 7 6 5 4 3 2 1

Copyright © 2012 by RotoVision SA

Manufactured in China

ISBN: 978 1 84543 429 8

Art Director: Emily Portnoi
Cover Design: Emily Portnoi
Design: Alphabetical
Commissioning Editor: Isheeta Mustafi

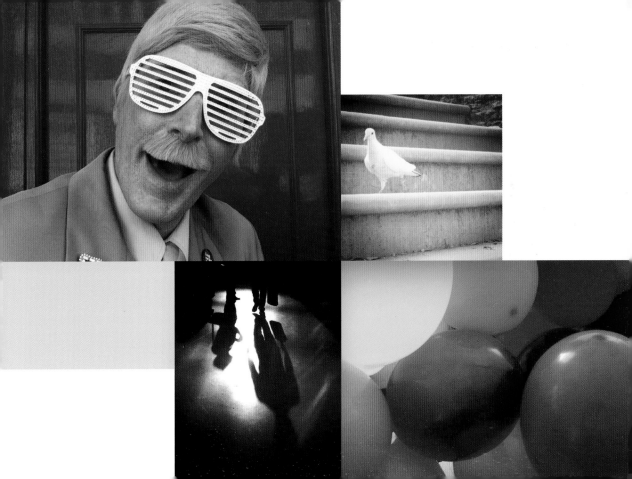

CONTENTS

INTRODUCTION

Almost every phone that's now sold, no matter how inexpensive, has a built-in camera. It used to be only photojournalists and a few others who went everywhere with a camera; now, it's all of us.

The Indian Ocean earthquake and tsunami in 2004 was the first global event where ordinary people with camera phones provided the majority of the first-day news footage. Professional news crews and photographers took longer to get on the scene. In 2007, the mayor of New York actively encouraged people to use their phones to capture pictures of crimes as they happened, and send them directly to 911.

We use phones to shoot the everyday, as well as the extraordinary. We use them as a tool to remember details by, snapping images of things we may need to refer to later on. And we have a whole photography studio in the palms of our hands. We can shoot a photo, edit it, and share it with anyone almost instantaneously—even if they're on the other side of the world.

This is the biggest revolution to happen in photography for some time.

As phones and the cameras in them get more sophisticated, the software application, or app, has emerged to open up yet more possibilities. Apps dramatically enhance a phone camera's basic functionality, and can take your photography to an exciting new level.

If you need your phone's camera to do something, chances are there'll be an app for it.

There are apps to help you shoot, apps for editing, apps to learn with, and apps that enhance creativity. They're cheap, many of

Your phone camera is the camera you always have with you, so it's ideal for capturing everyday scenes.

them are free, and they're really fun to use. Many apps are covered in this book, but it wasn't written to be a definitive list of what's out there. Things will date or be upgraded; new apps are coming out all the time. The idea is to help you discover the wonderful world of phone photography through some basic techniques and methods. I've tried to give starting points for the three main operating systems—Apple, Windows, and Android—where possible. Where I mention an app, it's assumed it's for the iPhone, unless I say otherwise.

But even if you don't have a phone that can run apps, I still think you'll find this book useful. If this book inspires you to try photography, whether on a phone or a traditional camera, then I'll be more than happy.

1 A filter accessory can lift your photos out of the ordinary.
2 Use editing apps to add interesting effects.
3 & 6 Apps such as Instagram allow you to shoot, edit, and upload your images to the Internet within minutes. Photo 3: Sarah Lawrence. Photo 6: Kevin Lawrence.
4 & 5 Apps can recreate the look of traditional camera and film types.
7 Tilt-shift apps can be used effectively for architectural photography.
8 Experiment with your phone camera's flash.

BEFORE THE SHOT

UNDERSTANDING YOUR PHONE'S CAMERA

It's a good idea to learn the basics about the camera in your phone so that you can work within its limits.

If you think about a traditional camera, whether a DSLR (digital single-lens reflex) or a compact point-and-shoot, it's been designed with one purpose: to take the best picture it can. Everything has gone into achieving that goal. There's so much more space in a digital camera to include the best components, the best lens, and the best possible functionality. A phone's prime purpose, however, is to be a communication device—the camera function is secondary. Phones are getting smaller and smaller, so the camera element of your phone has to be squeezed into a tiny space along with everything else.

Lens

The lens on the iPhone is only 5mm across. Compare that with the lens on a DSLR, which can be over 10 times wider than this. Most phone lenses have a fixed focal point, which means they don't have an optical zoom. (They do have a digital zoom, but that only zooms in on the image and degrades quality.)

Phones spend a lot of time in pockets, cases, and bags, and they can pick up lots of dust, marks, and especially fingerprints. So it's a good idea to clean your lens once in a while with a soft cloth, like the ones you get with sunglasses.

Sensor

The digital sensor in your phone camera captures the image, in the same way that film does in an analog camera. The sensor in your phone is smaller than the ones used in dedicated cameras, which can be a limitation in certain lighting conditions (see page 16).

Shutter

On a dedicated camera, like a DSLR, a shutter is a device inside the camera, rather like a curtain, which opens and closes to expose the sensor or film to light. On a phone camera, there's no physical shutter like this. There is, however, a shutter button that you press to take the shot. There is often a slight "shutter lag," or delay, between pressing the shutter button and the camera actually taking the photo.

Your phone's camera is never going to be able to take the same quality images that a dedicated camera can. Mostly, you'll notice this in low-light situations. But don't be put off by this. It's surprising what your phone's camera is capable of. There are so many truly beautiful images that are taken every day using phones. Just know the limits, work within them, and use them to your advantage.

DIFFERENT LIGHTING SITUATIONS

Photography is all about capturing light, and phone cameras perform better in certain lighting situations.

Because your phone has a small sensor (see page 14), any images taken in poor light won't be of the best quality. You'll notice digital noise, or a loss of definition (see page 56 on how to shoot in low light).

Shooting in bright light can be just as tricky. Phone cameras don't handle a big range of lighting situations that well: their small sensors can't capture a wide latitude of exposure levels. So if you're shooting someone with harsh sunlight hitting their face from the side, you may find that one side of their face is underexposed while the other is overexposed. Try to balance this by placing your subject in even light: turn them so that their face is either in the sun completely, or totally in the shade.

Every type of phone camera differs slightly, and as the technology improves, so will the quality of the images these cameras produce. The best way to find out what your camera is capable of is to actually use it. So go out and shoot in different lighting situations, and become a better photographer by knowing how to get the most out of your camera.

Shooting into the light can sometimes create strange effects.

Top Tip
If you're inside and taking photos, switch
the lights on. This should help illuminate
what you're taking a photo of, and will give
you a better chance of capturing a good-
quality image.

These images all show
how camera phones
work in different
lighting situations.

		2		6
1				5
	3	4		

1 I saw this beautiful light, then waited 10 minutes for the shadows to appear. If the light is right, use it, even if it means waiting longer to get the shot.

2 & 6 Experiment shooting outdoors on overcast days.

3 Get your subject to face the light to avoid harsh shadows.

4 Don't be afraid to shoot in dark situations.

5 This shot was lit by firing camera flashes at the subject, timing the flashes to coincide with the phone's shutter.

TAKING
THE
SHOT

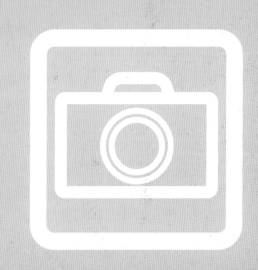

COMPOSITION AND GUIDELINES

Composition is one of the four elements of a really good photo, along with subject, exposure, and timing. There are various rules, tricks, and tips that you can use to make composing a photo easier.

Artists have known about the rules of composition for centuries. You can see these in evidence in many masterpieces, especially those from the Renaissance period. The "rule of thirds," especially, can really take your photography to the next level.

The rule works like this: Imagine your frame is divided into three equal vertical columns. Now, divide your frame into three equal horizontal rows. You should now have a grid consisting of nine sections. Think about where these sections cross. If you place anything of interest at the crossover points, you're using the rule of thirds, and your photos will benefit from it.

Various apps provide compositional guides like this, and actually overlay a grid onto your screen. Take a look at apps like Gorillacam, QuikCam, qbro (Android), and Camera Genius.

Create striking images by following the rule of thirds and placing your subject at the crossover points of the imaginary grid.

Things just look better when they're in threes, so think about using the power of three in your photos. Groups of people often look better if there's an odd number of them.

Top Tip
Other compositional tools you can use are leading lines (lines in the image that draw the viewer's eye into the picture) and diagonal composition. Diagonal compositions or lines can add a sense of drama to your images.

These apps make learning the rules of great photo composition a breeze.

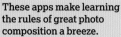

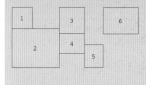

1 Get down low for a different viewpoint.
2 The small size of phones means you can take photos from unusual angles.
3 Arrange your subjects in groups of three. This often makes a better composition.
4 Try to include people walking into the shot. This will lead the viewer's eye into the image.
5 You can also use leading lines to draw the viewer's eye in.
6 The subject doesn't always have to be in the center of the image—an offcenter composition suits this quirky subject.

FOCUSING AND EXPOSURE

Focus and exposure are usually handled automatically on your phone's camera, but if you learn the principles behind each, it will really help your photography.

Focus

Most phone cameras have a big depth of field, so much of a scene will appear in focus. A shallow depth of field, on the other hand, will throw a background out of focus.

Usually, you focus in on a subject by tapping the corresponding part of the screen. Many shooting apps have this feature. But if you want your images to have a shallow depth of field, you'll probably need to change this after the image has been taken, with apps like iDOF, Photo FX, or iQuickD.O.F. SynthCam, however, does have a rather clever way of creating this effect while shooting. There are also many apps that can act as depth-of-field calculators (see page 180 for more on this).

Hold the camera steady and focus on the area of interest.

Exposure

Phone cameras usually take an exposure reading from the very center of the frame. However, you can change your image by altering where in the frame the camera exposes. For example, a scene with a wide range of highlights and lots of darkness can be shot in several ways. Take a look at the gallery on page 29 to see one image exposed in three different ways.

Some focus and exposure apps aren't that sensitive. To get things just right, it's well worth shooting with an app where you can set the exposure and the focus separately—this will give you more control over the image. Try apps like Camera+, ProCamera, and Focus Plus.

Top Tip
Think about where in the frame you want the viewer to look, and focus your camera on that. With exposure, it's always a good idea to focus on the "highlights," so expose for the brightest part of the frame. That way, you'll avoid a common problem with phone cameras: overexposed shots.

With these apps, you've got much more scope to adjust the focus and exposure of your photography.

1 If your subject is positioned offcenter, you'll need to adjust the focus point.
2 & 3 Don't be afraid to overexpose your shot—experiment with the effect. Photo 2: Kim Dale.
4–6 The same shot taken with three different exposures. 4 was exposed for the shadows, so the bright areas are too bright. 5 was exposed for the highlights, so the dark areas are too dark. 6 was a general exposure, so the dark and light areas are balanced.
7 Look for areas of light falling on your subject.
8 Self-portrait taken in a mirrored elevator. The mirrors reflected the light around the space.

FLASH

Many phones have a built-in flash, which can be really useful, but there are a few ways you can make it work for you better. If you feel the flash is making your shots too bright, try covering it with a small piece of paper to soften the effect. Also, use your flash sparingly. You don't have to keep it on Auto all the time; only switch it on when you need it.

The flash may have a red-eye function, which fires a quick burst of light before the shot is taken. This is supposed to help your subject's eyes become accustomed to the flash. It's worth switching this off, though, as it can delay the shot. It's far better to get an image with a little bit of red-eye than to miss the shot altogether.

If you have an iPhone, take a look at the Hipstamatic app, which allows you to change the color of the flash. You can also buy different types of flashes for this app.

There are various apps that are styled as flash apps, such as Night Shot, Camera Flash PRO Effects, and Camera Magic (Android). The majority of these only add a flash-type effect after the shot has been taken, although this can improve a dark image. Low-light apps are covered on page 56.

Take lots of portraits to experiment with your phone's flash.

Have you ever thought about using flash during the daytime? Try it on a bright, sunny day to "fill in" the shadows on a portrait. Your subject may have half their face in shadow, and by just adding a little burst of flash, you can reduce the shadow and get a better picture.

Top Tip
When you're using flash, anything else in the shot that's reflective will light up like a Christmas tree. Either avoid using it, or work with it for creative effect.

With some apps you can change the color of the flash; with others you can add flash effects during editing.

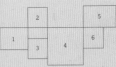

1 & 3 Using flash is a great way to to shoot a night out with friends.
2 & 4 Switching off the red-eye function means you get more spontaneous shots.
5 Anything reflective, such as the silver hat in this photo, will be lit up by the flash.
6 Use flash to freeze your subject. This is particularly useful when photographing children as they usually don't want to sit still for very long.

INTERVAL SHOOTING, TIME-LAPSE, AND SELF-TIMERS

Apps like Gorillacam, Camera Genius, Burst Mode, Photo Timer, and Vignette (Android) allow you to shoot a number of pictures over a span of time. With multiple images, you can tell more of a story than you can with just one. These apps are a great way of adding creativity to your photography.

Interval Shooting
Say you're shooting a fast-moving object, like a racing car. Interval shooting really works here, using a quick burst of photos to capture movement. Try also changing the position of your camera in between shots.

Time-Lapse
You're watching a beautiful sunset. Use time-lapse to take a shot every 30 seconds for 60 shots, recording the movement of the sun over half an hour. Animate the shots on your computer later, to create a little movie of the sun setting.

Self-Timers
Great for self-portraits, including yourself in group shots, or any photo where you need to keep the camera steady. A tripod of some kind is handy (see page 212). Once your camera is in place, set the shutter to fire. Give yourself enough time to get into the shot—at least 10 seconds. Set it for 2 seconds if you just want to keep the camera steady.

Some of the apps mentioned above have self-timers, as well as Camera Self Timer (Android) and Self Timer.

Self-timers mean you can include yourself in the family portrait.

Top Tip
Have a go at time-lapse shooting—it can be great fun. Think about shooting something that's going to change over a period of time. Think about the end result of your little film; create an animation of something interesting.

These apps allow you to capture multiple images over a period of time, which is ideal for telling stories.

| 1 | 2 | 3 | 4 |
| 5 | | 6 | |

1–4 These photos were taken using a four-shot interval sequence.
5 Multiple images were taken using a continuous shooting mode to ensure that one shot perfectly captured a mid-air jump. Photo: Emily Portnoi.
6 This was taken using a self-timer and a fish-eye lens, with the phone hoisted up on a tripod to get the overhead shot.

SPIRIT LEVEL
AND ARCHITECTURAL
PHOTOGRAPHY

When it comes to taking pictures of buildings or landscapes, it's really important to get your lines level. Nothing spoils a beautiful image like a crooked horizon. After all, this is how we usually see the world.

Try to get your verticals vertical, too. Make sure your buildings don't look like they're about to fall over. The same applies to indoor photography—try not to make it look like you were drunk when you took the shot.

Apps that can help you get your lines level include Grid Cam, Gorillacam, ProCamera, and Retro Camera Plus (Android). These all have a built-in digital spirit level that uses the phone's accelerometer. I wouldn't recommend using it for any real building work, but the spirit level can come in very handy when you're shooting. Use it with a tripod (see page 212) to get your images spot on, or when holding the camera normally.

If you do get a slightly crooked shot, don't worry. It's also possible to crop and straighten your images with a range of apps (see page 96).

Taking a shot of a building from an unusual angle can create some quite abstract results.

Most phone lenses are fairly wide-angle, so you'll always get some distortion of perspective. When shooting, make sure the most prominent lines in your images are straight. Think about which ones you notice first, and make sure they line up. This should give you the best image. You can even try using the wide angle of the lens to get unusual angles and perspectives.

A Professional View
If you're going to photograph buildings, think about the inside of them as well as the outside. The interior may be far more interesting. Also, think about the time of day. Dusk, just when the sky turns dark blue and the lights come on, is a perfect time to shoot architecture.

These apps can all help you shoot more accurate horizontals and verticals.

1	3		4		6	8
2				5		7

1 & 2 Look out for objects that are out of scale.
3 Get your camera low down for a different view of an urban landscape.
4 & 6 Wherever you place it in the shot, getting the horizon line straight will make for a better landscape. Photo 4: Will Scobie.
5 When shooting inside a building, don't forget to look up—there may be interesting details that you'd otherwise miss.
7 Getting lines straight can be important when shooting portraits, too.
8 After dark is a great time to photograph cityscapes. Photo: Leanne Coe.

TOUCH ANYWHERE AND ANTI-SHAKE

Using your camera's shutter button can be tricky sometimes. It's not always in the most convenient place, and sometimes it's tiny, so you end up fumbling for it and missing shots.

A multitude of shooting apps like Gorillacam, Camera Genius, and Big Camera Button (Android) allow you to tap anywhere on the screen to take a photo. This can make things easier, but be aware that some apps sacrifice the ability to focus and expose by having this function.

Anti-shake apps like 1Shoot, Camera+, Anti-Shake Camera, and Vignette (Android) use the camera's accelerometer to help with image stabilization, so there should be no excuse for getting a blurry picture. These apps take the picture automatically when you're holding the phone steady. Some apps like Gorillacam actually have a little gauge that tells you when you're steady enough to shoot.

This means that it can take slightly longer to take the photo, but you need to decide what you want from your image. A bit of blur can sometimes add to the artistic feel of the shot.

Anti-shake is a useful option for taking a clear image when you don't have a tripod with you.

A Professional View

To avoid shake and blur in their images, professionals often use a tripod and self-timer to take their photos. Take a look at the section on accessories on page 194.

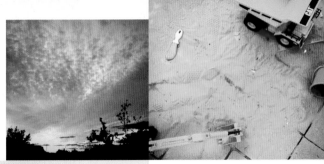

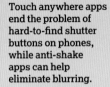

Touch anywhere apps end the problem of hard-to-find shutter buttons on phones, while anti-shake apps can help eliminate blurring.

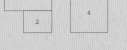

1 & 6 These photos were taken in shadow, so anti-shake apps helped to stabilize them.
2 & 3 With babies and fast-moving animals, you need to take the photo fast, so touch-anywhere apps are a great option.
4 This was taken on a windy day. An anti-shake app meant I could photograph the moving branches and avoid blur.
5 This beautiful sunset photo was achieved using an anti-shake app with a makeshift tripod. Photo: Jeremy Long.

MULTIPLE EXPOSURE

Multiple exposure is where you overlay two or more shots to create a unique, multi-layered image. Multiple Exposure Creator (Android), OXCamera, and BlendCam can all give you this very creative effect, and these apps are all subtly different from one another.

Consider how many shots you need in a multiple exposure image. The more you take, the more detail you capture. However, this can cause problems, as you're essentially exposing the shot over and over. You may end up capturing too much light, resulting in a very white or overblown image.

BlendCam has a very handy tool for this, allowing you to shoot in Balance mode. Here, the software balances the image to give a correct exposure, no matter how many shots you take—something a normal camera can't do.

Think about how the final, combined image will look. You don't want it to be a big mess, which unfortunately is a common outcome of multiple exposure shots.

Multiple exposures work best when they are kept simple.

Try to introduce some pattern into your multiple exposure images, as repeating these can work well. Try flipping one of your shots, so that you create a mirror image in your frame. Another idea is to juxtapose two shots in one image for impact.

Take the same shot several times, while slightly twisting the camera to create a kind of drunken, hazy feel.

Multiple exposure is a great way to get creative with portraits: try placing your subject's head in different positions in the frame. Look for patterns or textures that will add interest to your portrait.

With these apps, it's all about layering one photo over another to create something beautiful.

1–4 Multiple exposures add interest to portraits. Photo 3: Kevin Birk.
5 Try flipping your phone around and taking the same shot twice.
6 The use of multiple exposures gives this image a ghostly, atmospheric feel.
7 Get creative and mix your shots to create surreal images.

MACRO PHOTOGRAPHY

Macro photography is defined as close-up photography of very small subjects. Professional photographers use specialized lenses and equipment to capture this view of the world, but it's also possible with phones.

At the moment, it's very difficult to get an app to help with macro photography, as no app will make your camera focus any closer than it already can. However, the good news is that your camera can probably focus pretty close to objects already. Give it a go. Just make sure that you hold your camera steady, and use the tap to focus feature (see page 26) to get sharp images.

Another way to get even closer to your subject is to use a specialized close-up lens adapter (see page 196). You can even use a standard magnifying glass, or any type of lens that you can hold in front of your camera.

Test your phone's focus by experimenting with macro photography.

If you know your subject won't move, try using a tripod (see page 212) and a self-timer app, as you'll find that any slight movement at this distance will affect focus. Be aware that you may block a lot of the light on your subject with your hand and phone being so close, so pick a bright spot—or think about adding your own light from the sides.

If you can't quite get close enough to your subject, try pulling the camera back and focus right in with the digital zoom. You'll lose image quality, as you're zooming in on the actual pixels, not the subject. But this technique can work very well.

Show a totally different view of the world and get super close-up using adapters, lenses, or the zoom function.

1	3		5	7
2		4	6	

1 & 3 Approach animals slowly to avoid startling them and making them move.
2 Shooting macro images helps you develop an eye for unusual viewpoints.
4 Look out for interesting details on large subjects.
5 Zooming in close means you will lose some image quality.
6 & 7 Macro shots of flowers and cakes can have a romantic feel. Photo 6: Laura Baab. Photo 7: Sarah Lawrence.

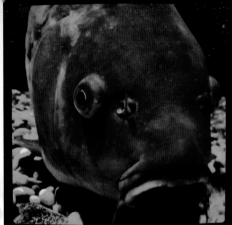

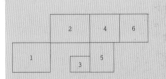

| | 2 | 4 | 6 |
| 1 | 3 | 5 | |

1–5 When shooting macro, be aware of the light falling on your subject as you need to avoid having too much contrast. Use direct sunlight (photos 2 and 5), shoot in the shadows (photo 1), or shoot indoors (photos 3 and 4). **6** This was taken indoors using the internal light of the fish tank to light the subject.

LOW LIGHT

The fundamental ingredient in any image is the light that's been captured. It's no secret that the cameras in most phones aren't as good as dedicated professional cameras. So phone cameras tend to work best in bright environments. But what happens if you're shooting in a low-light situation?

Actually, you'll be surprised how well your phone can cope. It's still possible to take photos even in very dark conditions. Sure, the quality of the images may be poor, but you can still capture something very usable.

The main issue you'll encounter in low-light photography is digital noise. This is the variation of brightness and color in individual pixels, caused by the way the phone's digital sensors handle dark situations. However, apps such as Photoshop Express (iPhone and Android) have a noise-reduction filter, where you can correct this problem after the shot.

If you're looking for an app to help you shoot in low light, take a look at Darkroom, NightVision Pro, Night Camera, and Snap Photo Pro (Android).

Low-light portraits can be very atmospheric.

If you're interested in night photography, try light painting. With a slow shutter-speed exposure, any movement of light will be captured as a streak across your frame—for example, a passing car's headlights. For this technique, look at apps like Slow Shutter Cam.

With apps like Light Painting and Camera Streak (Android), you use your phone as the light source and paint with that. For something more advanced, try an app like Penki, where you can input words to be displayed over images, captured through movement and long exposure.

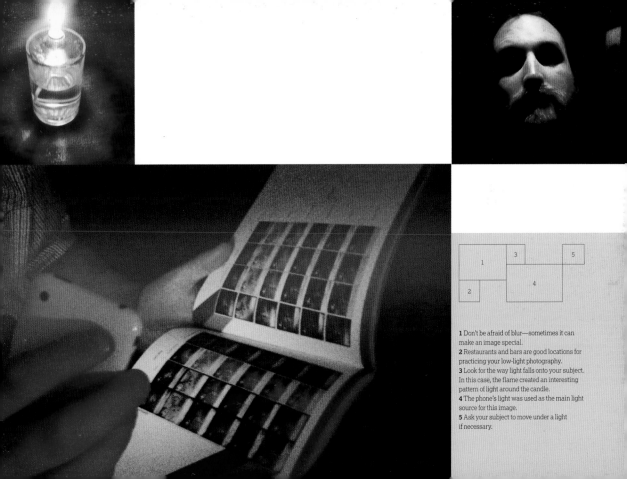

1 Don't be afraid of blur—sometimes it can make an image special.
2 Restaurants and bars are good locations for practicing your low-light photography.
3 Look for the way light falls onto your subject. In this case, the flame created an interesting pattern of light around the candle.
4 The phone's light was used as the main light source for this image.
5 Ask your subject to move under a light if necessary.

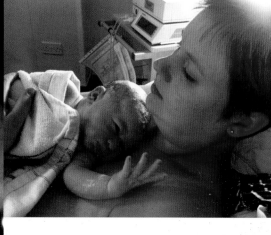

There are apps that can improve image quality when shooting in low light, and apps that reduce digital noise after the shot. Use them, too, for long exposures and light painting.

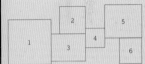

1 The streaks of bright light on the floor add some sparkle to this shot.
2 You might not get perfect images of the performers, but you can certainly capture the atmosphere of a concert. Photo: Selena Goldsmith.
3 This was taken a few minutes after my daughter was born. Take your camera phone everywhere and you'll never miss a shot.
4 This portrait was shot outdoors at night using the phone's flash: Photo: Jeremy Long.
5 The blur you get with low light can add to the sense of movement in a shot.
6 Expose for the light areas in a shot. If this had been exposed for the dark areas, the colored lights would have been too bright and blown out.

PANORAMIC AND 360

A panoramic photo is usually an image that's captured with an elongated field of vision. We're used to seeing images from camera phones in a standard format, or ratio. However, a panoramic image is much wider than this.

Normally, to capture a panoramic image, you need specialized cameras or sophisticated software to stitch your images together. Apps like Pano, PanoPhoto (Android), PanoLab, 360 Panorama, AutoStitch, and Ztitch (Windows) can all do the hard work for you.

So if you see a fantastic vista, which you just can't capture with a normal photo, think about using an app to shoot it all. Some apps guide you through the process by telling you where to shoot; others let you decide.

Don't be afraid of broken images—sometimes these can work well, especially when shooting an iconic subject.

Some apps help you line up the shots as you're shooting, and some let you overlay and stitch the shots together after the event. Try to keep the camera in roughly the same position for each image—otherwise, any variation will show when you stitch the images together, and they may not line up. That is, of course, unless you want to play around and create a kind of cubist shot.

Think outside the box about your subject matter. Sure, a landscape will work well as a panoramic image. But why not try an urban scene, or even a unique portrait?

1	2
3	

1 & 2 Panoramic apps allow you to capture an entire landscape on your phone.
3 Indoor scenes can also make great subjects for panoramas.

1	4
2	
3	5

1 A panoramic is an ideal way to capture a special occasion. This crowd scene was taken in London on the wedding day of Prince William and Catherine Middleton.
2 & 3 Look out for interesting urban scenes, such as large areas of street art or people gathered in parks.
4 Try a panoramic rather than a standard group portrait.
5 Think in 360. Does your location look great all around you?

These apps give you the
chance to take a wider view
with your photography.

	2			5
1	3	4		

1 Don't just think in terms of landscapes, portraits can work well too, although you'll probably find that this will take a bit of practice before you get it right.

2 & 3 Crowd scenes work well as panoramics.

4 Stitch images together to include more of the foreground in a landscape.

5 Try out panoramics for still-life subjects as well as landscapes.

HDR

You may have seen the term "HDR" on your phone's settings, which stands for High Dynamic Range. HDR uses image-processing software to show a greater tonal range between the lightest and darkest areas of an image.

Think about how you see the world. You may look at a street scene and see that one side of the street is in shadow and the other side is in bright sunlight. Your eyes will see detail on both sides of the street. However, a digital camera isn't able to see the world in such great detail or latitude of exposure tones. Most digital cameras will expose for the highlights, the mid-tones, or the shadows. So usually, lots of detail in your image will be lost.

In HDR mode, the camera takes a few different exposures of the same subject, and combines these to create one image with a higher dynamic range.

Some phones have an HDR function built in, but there are apps available too, some of which are Pro HDR, TrueHDR, Pro HDR (Android), and Camera 360 Pro (Android).

Bold, plain colors make good backdrops for HDR portraits.

Top Tip
It'll take much longer to shoot with an HDR app, as the camera needs to take three photos and combine them, so if you're in a hurry, this won't be for you. Also, be very careful not to over-process your pictures. Try to make your HDR images look like the real world. Some people go over the top with their HDR processing, and the images look ridiculously unnatural.

HDR apps can boost the range of exposure tones for a shot, giving your image much more definition.

| 1 | | 3 | | 6 |
| 2 | | 4 | 5 | |

1–3 The sky can look great if shot correctly using HDR. Look out for an interesting sky, rather than one that is just one color.
4 & 5 Shooting HDR takes longer, so stationary subjects are ideal, especially when you're learning the technique.
6 When I saw this man in the street, I just had to take his photo. HDR apps mean you'll never miss an opportunity for a colorful portrait.

MULTIPLE LENSES

Multi-lens cameras take several images on the same frame. Generally, they fall into the category of toy cameras (see page 132). They can be great fun to shoot with, and produce some really unusual and interesting images. Some cameras split the frame into four, either vertically or in quarters. Some divide a shot into eight, and some even have 16 images on the frame.

These cameras either take the images over a short time span, like two seconds, or they shoot them all simultaneously.

Several apps mimic what multi-lens cameras do. The good news is that they allow you to be really in control of your final image. You can change the settings in the apps to shoot four, eight, or 16 images in one frame. You may also be able to change the timing of when the image is taken. This means you can take all the images at the same time, or over a period of a few seconds, depending on what you think will work best. You can really have fun with your shots, and even tell a little story with your final image.

Take a look at apps like MultiCamera (Android), QuadCamera and Fotomecha to start with, and see what works for you.

Add interest to still-life shots by using a multi-lens app.

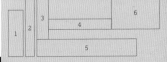

1 & 4 Include people in your scene to tell a
story. Photo 4: Emily Portnoi.
2 Use a multi-lens app as a way to capture
a whole landscape.
3 Have fun by mixing up the angles.
5 Look for subjects that include repeated
patterns. This will add extra impact to a
multi-lens image.
6 Experiment with multi-lens apps for portraits.

RETRO CAMERAS

For some reason, we want our phone photos to look like they were taken with vintage film cameras. It's a very popular technique that can look great, but if you think about it, it's also quite puzzling: phone photography is probably one of the most recent revolutions in image-making, and we want its results to look distinctly old-school.

There's nothing in the rulebook that says this is how it has to be done. In fact, there isn't a rulebook at all. If you don't like it, fine; if you do like it, keep on doing it.

It's possible to take retro-style photos with apps like Retro Camera (Android), Hipstamatic, Hipstar (Windows), and Vignette (Android). There are many different camera-type apps, and half the fun is seeing which one works for you.

It's always worth comparing these shooting apps with apps where you can edit your shot after the event (see page 112). Try film-type apps (see page 118) for similar analog effects.

Add a vintage feel to a modern scene with a retro camera app.

HPSTM 269

These apps simulate the classic analog qualities of vintage camera photography.

| 1 | | 3 | | 5 | 7 |
| 2 | | | 4 | 6 | |

1–4 Look for timeless subjects that work well with the vintage look.

5 Select a retro camera app to shoot an event to give your photos a theme. This was taken at a wedding where everything, including the transport, had a vintage theme. Photo: Emily Portnoi.

6 & 7 Retro-camera apps can also work well with urban and architectural photography.

M 269 HPS

HPSTM 269

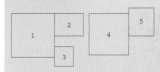

1 This temple is another great example
of a timeless subject.
2 However, don't be afraid to play around
with your subject matter. This shot combines
the retro-camera effect with some modern
street art.
3 This old truck was an ideal subject for
a vintage-style shot.
4 Don't forget to look up, wherever you are!
5 A retro-camera app is a great choice for
a romantic portrait.

FILM TYPES

There are so many different film types available, it would be impossible to list them all here. All you need to be aware of is that different films produce different effects. Low color-saturated film is good for skin tones, for example.

Black-and-white films vary hugely. You can get higher-contrast films for punchy shots with impact. Some films have lots of grain, which gives a distinctive feel to images. Other types include instant film, slide film, and medium-format film. These are covered in more detail on page 118.

Apps can either simulate different film types while shooting, or after the shot. It's far easier to edit a standard shot after you've taken it than it is to shoot a picture a particular way, as you'll have a lot more options. However, it's always worth experimenting with apps that shoot in different film formats. Try Hipstamatic, Vignette (Android), and Hipstar (Windows).

Film-type apps can recreate the look of instant-film photos.

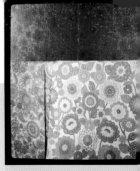

These apps can give you all the nuances and variety of analog film types.

		4	6		9
1	3				8
2		5		7	

1 Use black-and-white film apps to emphasise the contrast in your shots.

2 Keep an eye out for reflections in buildings—these can make great shots.

3 & 5–9 Apps can recreate the look of various film types, including 35mm slides (photo 3), full-bleed negatives (photo 5), cross-processed film (photo 6), medium-format (photos 7 and 8), and Fuji Instax Wide (photo 9).

4 These retro-print fabrics are a nice choice of subject for a film-type app.

GIMMICKS

"Gimmicks" in this context describes fun apps that don't really fit into any other kind of category, but the term isn't in any way meant to be negative. On the contrary, these apps can be the source of endless amusement.

There are apps that shoot images like they're taken in an old photo booth (IncrediBooth); apps that superimpose you on a very different background; apps that can put your facial features on someone else's head (OldBooth); and apps that give your friends "fat faces" (iFaceFat).

Trimensional is a great app that enables you to shoot a three-dimensional picture of someone's face. It takes a few different images of a face in quick succession, then uses software to combine them into a photo you can look at from different angles.

Another great app is called Everyday. It's based on the premise of taking a self-portrait every day; then it creates an animated video for you.

In fact, there are many apps that don't fit the categories covered in this book, too many to list here. Take a look on various websites like www.iphoneography.com, www.androinica.com, www.windowsphoneapplist.com, for reviews and news on the latest apps.

Face-swap apps work well with pictures of couples.

Half the fun of these apps is just discovering them and showing them to your friends and family. They can be really good fun to shoot with, and can get everyone laughing. So go explore—be the first of your friends to discover the next must-have app. Yes, you have to pay for them, but so what? Where else can you have this much fun for less than a dollar?

1–5 Apps that mimic photo booths are a lot of fun. Ask your subject to pull a different expression in each shot.

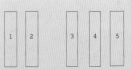

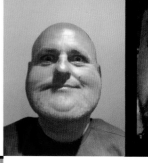

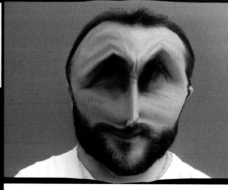

The great thing about these apps is the reactions you'll get from friends and family when you use them.

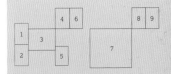

1 Apps make playing dress-up easy!
2, 6 & 9 Shoot 3D images in a dark environment to get the best results.
3, 4 & 7 Play around with apps that distort your subject's features.
5 & 8 Give portraits the look of old-fashioned high-school yearbook photos.

EDITING
THE
SHOT

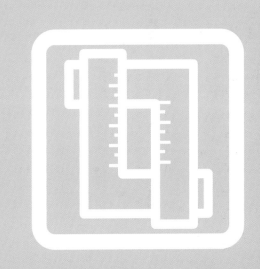

CROPPING, ROTATING, AND STRAIGHTENING

Sometimes, a picture you take isn't quite how you want it. The framing is wrong. Something on the edge of the shot is spoiling it. Your horizon isn't perfectly level. Or, thanks to the angle you held your phone at, its accelerometer has saved the image in portrait when you wanted landscape.

All of these niggles can be fixed with apps. PhotoGene, Cropulator, Photo Lab 1600, Adobe Photoshop Express (Android), Crop For Free, Thumba Photo Editor (Windows), and PhotoForge can all help you with after-the-shot editing.

When it comes to cropping and straightening, less really is more. The camera on your phone may not be able to capture the biggest image file or the most detail in a picture. So cropping or straightening your photo by any amount is going to reduce the image size, and with it, its definition. So try to crop and straighten as little as possible.

It's always best to get the image right when shooting, but if you do need a little helping hand, all is not lost with these apps.

Careful use of these apps will help you to perfect your compositions.

To straighten an image, use the function in your image-editing app and move the image to get it how you want it. Remember, the greater the angle of straightening, the smaller the final image will be.

Rotating your image should be fairly easy, and you shouldn't lose any image quality, but you should be able to view the image the right way around on your screen. It's also possible to flip your image, horizontally or vertically, if you need to.

Images look best if they're kept at the original ratios they were taken at. So a crazy crop to a long rectangle or other shape will look a little odd. Try a small crop or a square crop first.

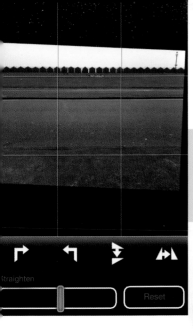

These apps help you edit your photos, so they're just the way you want them.

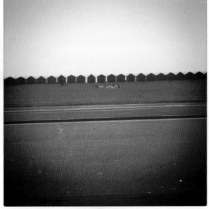

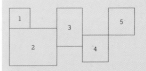

1 & 2 Crop in on your images to focus attention on key details.
3–5 The horizon should be level in a photograph. Use editing apps to straighten your lines.

EXPOSURE, CONTRAST, AND BRIGHTNESS

Phone cameras now feature highly advanced technology. But when it comes to capturing all the different tones of a scene, or getting the exposure right over a whole image, they still don't quite measure up to digital or film cameras.

If your image is a little dark, or looks too flat or overexposed, these apps can make it picture perfect. Start with Thumba Photo Editor (Windows), iRetouch, PicSay (Android), Snap Photo Pro (Android) and Photoshop.com Mobile. They all work a little differently, so experiment and find the one that works for you.

Exposure
This usually changes the whole exposure for the image, so it alters the highlights, mid-tones, and shadows. You can also alter specific settings for these features, so you don't have to change the whole image.

Contrast
If your image is a little flat and it could do with a bit of punch, consider changing the contrast of your shot.

Brightness
If you have detail in your entire image, but it looks a little dark or dull, try changing the brightness. This doesn't affect the exposure. It's worth looking at the exposure or contrast first, though.

This shot is underexposed, but that adds to the drama. If the sky were correctly exposed, the photo would not have the same mood.

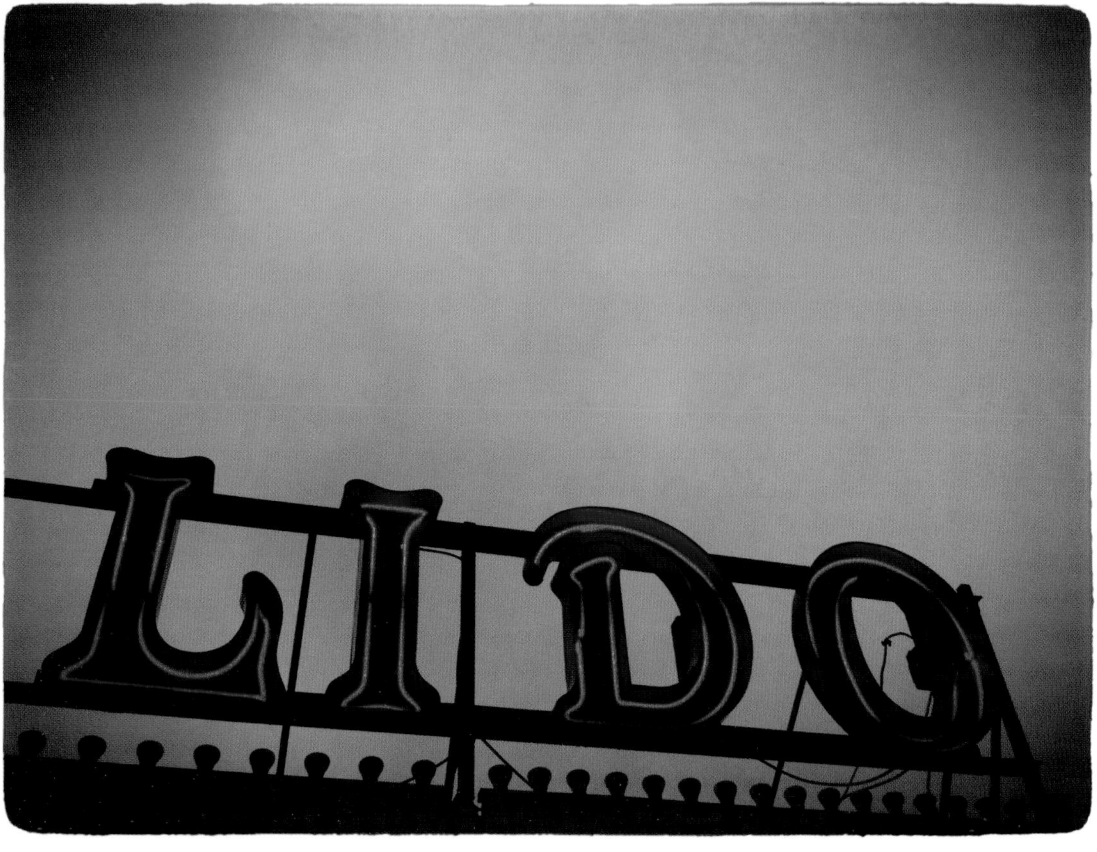
LIDO

If you're really pleased with the subject and composition of a shot, but the overall exposure's letting it down, change the contrast, brightness, or exposure to improve it. A systematic approach often helps here. Try changing one setting at a time and see what happens. It may be that you need to go back and alter one of them after you've changed another.

A Professional View

Photographers have always adjusted exposure, contrast, and brightness. In the past, it was done when making a print from a negative. If the image was too dark, you exposed the print paper a while longer. Now, with sophisticated image-editing software like Photoshop, there are very few professional images that haven't been altered in some way.

These apps help you adjust the exposure, contrast, and brightness in your shot to get the balance just right.

1 & 8 Adjust settings to add impact.
2 I edited the contrast and exposure to darken areas of this image. This helps lead the viewer's eye up the stairs to the light.
3 Experiment with settings to alter the mood of sky shots.
4 Editing the contrast can improve a well-composed shot. Photo: Laura Baab.
5 & 6 These photos are vastly overexposed, but they still work.
7 Play around with the exposure and contrast until you find the right balance of light falling onto your subject.
9 This was taken from a moving car, early in the morning. The dark exposure makes this shot successful.

COLOR CORRECTION

A camera lens sees the world differently from the human eye. That super-bright red you loved? Your camera may not quite have captured it. Or maybe the colors in your whole image are too dull or too intense. Different types of lights and lighting conditions can also have an effect.

White, in particular, can be one of the trickiest colors to capture. For example, see how a desk lamp may appear yellow or orange. A fluorescent light may look slightly green, and car headlamps may appear blue. The different tones from light sources can all affect your image's "color temperature."

To remedy this, check out apps such as Perfect Photo, Thumba Photo Editor (Windows), PhotoCurves, PicSay (Android), Photoshop.com Mobile (Android), and PhotoGene, which allow you to increase or decrease the color intensity of your shot.

By using apps, you can correct the colors to be closer to how you remembered them. You can change the whole image's color, or some apps give you the option to change specific colors, like greens or reds, which really gives you control.

The vibrant colors are what make this photo really successful.

When you're color correcting, think about what looks natural. Green or red skin tones just don't look good. If you want to experiment, then go for it, but aim for a great image, rather than making it unusual just for the sake of it.

A Professional View
If a photographer shot a sweater for a clothing retailer but the real thing looked nothing like its picture online, there'd be real problems. Professionals often take a shot of a specific color balance card, or mid-gray card, under the lighting conditions they're shooting in. At the editing stage they alter the mid-gray on the image to match the standard mid-gray on the card, thus ensuring a better color balance.

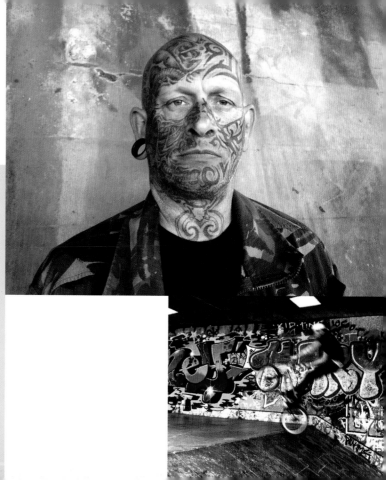

If you want to adjust the color of your pictures in any way, these apps are for you.

		3		6
	1			
			4	5
	2			

1 I kicked myself for walking past this man without taking his picture. So I went back and asked him for a quick photo. Editing the shot afterward helped to get his remarkable tattoo looking just right.
2–4 Apps can help you get intense colors in your shots. Photo 4: Emily Portnoi.
5 Be careful to keep skin tones looking natural when color correcting a portrait.
6 White is a difficult color to photograph, so an editing app is a good way to get it right in post-production.

BLACK-AND-WHITE CONVERSION

There's something so timeless and emotional about a monochrome photo. Black-and-white photography forces you to focus on the subject and composition of a picture, without the distractions that color can bring.

Henri Cartier-Bresson, the influential street photographer, used black-and-white to its full potential. Contemporary photographers often prefer mono images for portraits, fashion, and many other types of photography.

Apps that can help you convert your images to black-and-white include MonoPhix, Pictures Lab (Windows), Adobe Photoshop Express (Android), Vignette (Android), Cool fx, and PhotoForge.

Results will vary depending on the app. You'll find some converted images are black-heavy; some have lots of contrast, while others have very little. Some will have a slight yellow or a slight blue tone. Brightness, and the grays in an image, can vary too.

In the world of analog photography, different black-and-white films give different results. Some of them are particularly grainy, some have deep blacks, and some have great tonal ranges. So take a look at film-type emulator apps (see page 118) to discover a range of conversion effects.

You may want to desaturate (see page 104) your image and experiment with changing the levels and other aspects of the exposure yourself (see page 100) to have the most control.

Convert your color portraits to black and white to give them a different feel.

Start out with street photography (taking images of everyday life). Shooting in monochrome takes some of the information out of the image (as there's no color), so you're really forced to look at the world differently.

Think about tone, texture, and contrast. Does your subject look flat, or is there a great tonal range to the scene? A bright red or a bright blue may not look the same in black-and-white. Sometimes squinting at a subject can help you see tones more easily.

Try taking dramatic portraits, using shadows to give your subject impact. You'll soon train your monochrome eye to look for great images that have maximum impact.

These apps open up the world of black-and-white photography to create strong emotional impact and a wonderful sense of timelessness.

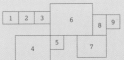

1	2	3		6		8	9
		4		5		7	

1–3 These three shots were taken at the same time, but they show how different the effects of black-and-white conversion can be.
4 & 8 Black and white works well for street photography.
5, 7 & 9 Convert your images to black and white to give them a timeless feel. Photo 5 & 9: Kevin Birk.
6 Shooting into the light created a silhouette. This strong contrast made this photo suitable for converting to black and white.

CAMERA TYPES

There are a whole host of apps to make your images look like they were shot with a particular type of camera. Some examples are Pictures Lab (Windows), CameraBag, Retro Camera (Android), SwankoLab, Vignette (Android), and Free Photo Filters. Usually they apply lo-fi effects, such as texture or blur, but it all depends on the specific app.

Camera types that are simulated by apps include:

• 35mm and medium-format: the two most common types of film cameras

• Toy (see page 132): plastic and lo-fi cameras

• Instant (see page 122): Polaroid and others

• Vintage: classic, older cameras

• Multi-lens (see page 74): takes multiple shots, combining them into one image

• Fish-eye: gives a distorted view, like you're looking through a goldfish bowl

It's often easier to use camera-type apps after the shot, at the editing stage. You'll have more time to experiment, and you'll have the benefit of keeping the original image and working on a copy. In fact, you can work on as many copies and try as many camera types as you like. When you shoot with a camera-type app, you generally just have that image. Some apps save an original, but you don't have the option to see what your image will look like with this camera or that camera.

Apps can recreate the look of a photo taken using a 35mm camera.

A Professional View

I tend to use the camera type I think is right for the shoot. I really enjoy shooting with lots of different film cameras, but if it's a serious job for a client, I'll shoot with a high-end digital SLR—unless, of course, I can persuade the client that a film camera will work better for their needs. If you apply this principle when selecting different camera types to shoot and edit, you shouldn't go far wrong.

With these apps, you can emulate different camera types, like Polaroids or toy cameras, with endless scope for experimenting.

| 1 | | 3 | | 5 |
| 2 | | | 4 | |

1–3 & 5 Editing apps can recreate the look of various camera types, including medium-format cameras (photos 1 and 5), Lomo/toy cameras (photo 2), and Polaroids (photo 3).
4 This is a modified Holga camera, also known as a toy camera.

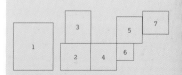

```
      ┌────┐   ┌────────┐
      │    │   │   3    │   ┌──────┐  ┌────┐
┌─────┴──┐ │   │        │   │  5   │  │ 7  │
│        │ │   └────────┤   │      │  │    │
│   1    │ │   ┌───┐┌───┤───┤  ┌───┴──┤    │
│        │ │   │ 2 ││ 4 │   │  │  6   │    │
└────────┘ │   └───┘└───┘   └──┤      └────┘
```

1–7 The camera types used here include
Polaroid (photo 1), 35mm (photo 2), Lomo/toy
camera (photos 3, 6, and 7), and medium
format (photos 4 and 5). Photo 5: Emily Portnoi.

FILM TYPES

Just as there are apps that simulate different cameras (see page 112), there are others that recreate different film types, including some that are no longer available. SwankoLab, Lo-Mob, PictureShow, FxCamera (Android), and CameraBag are just some examples of these apps. These are the types of film you can recreate:

35mm
Shot in a 3 × 2 ratio, 35mm gives a rectangular image. This may differ from the photo your camera takes—so it may be cropped. 35mm apps can emulate the popular technique of "shooting the sprockets"— where the image runs to the whole width of the film, including the sprocket holes.

120
Also known as medium-format film, this shoots mainly square images. Still used by professional and amateur photographers,

it gives great detail. Many vintage cameras used this film, so some vintage-effect apps will emulate 120 film.

Slide Film
This produces a positive rather than a negative strip of images. Usually characterized by the white holder around the slides, this film isn't popular in the digital age, but apps can emulate it.

Infrared
This film captures light wavelengths outside the normal spectrum of the human eye. Generally black-and-white, the images will have an unusual look and feel to them: the sky can be black, and trees can have white leaves. See pages 108 and 122 for black-and-white and instant-film effects.

This photo was edited with a film-type app. In this case, the app recreated the look of black-and-white high-contrast film.

You'll be surprised how different your image can look in all of these film formats. Your photo may not work as an instant print, but converting it to infrared might be just what it needs to really make it pop.

Experiment by editing your photos with different film types. Get used to the effects they produce, and you'll start to see your image opportunities differently. Be careful to choose a film type that works with the shot, and not just for the sake of it.

By using film-type apps, you can create a sense of nostalgia and give your images that something extra they need.

UN 60T6

	2		5
1	3	4	6

1 The composition of this shot lends itself to the addition of film sprockets.
2–6 Apps can recreate the look of various film types, including high-grain black-and-white film (photo 2), medium-format print film with borders (photo 3), slide film (photo 4), Fuji Instax wide film (photo 5), and medium format with light leaks (photo 6).

INSTANT
FILM

You probably know how to "shake it like a Polaroid picture." But did you know that Polaroid doesn't make film anymore? Since the last factory closed its doors, the film has been resurrected (in a very experimental way) by a group of former Polaroid employees in a brave venture called The Impossible Project.

That's good news for film users, but there are also various apps, such as ShakeItPhoto, Polarize, Apict (Windows), Retro Camera (Android), and roidizer (Android) that act as "fauxlaroids" on phone cameras. In other words, they simulate many of the effects of instant film that are so loved, like the classic white border of instant film.

These apps aren't just limited to simulating Polaroid film. There are instant films made by Fuji that have alternative size images; apps are available for these. Even for Polaroid film, different apps do it in different ways.

You may get pictures with nice, uniform borders, while other apps give your images messy edges. Some even copy the way the image develops on instant film, with your shots appearing onscreen slowly before your eyes. You can also buy apps that replicate instant peel-apart film. These have a very different feel from the standard instant films.

The instant-film look works best with an image that has a square format.

When editing your images to look like instant-film pictures, be aware that the format is usually square. You need to take this into account when shooting, as some of the image will be cropped. Take a look at this gallery, see which images you like, and start experimenting along those lines.

These apps recreate the feel and effects of instant-film types.

1 Choose colorful subjects. These will provide a nice contrast to the white border.
2 Get in close to your subject.
3 Include areas of negative space to add balance to your compositions.
4 Shoot the everyday—there are good photos all around you.
5 Some apps add messy borders, which can add interest to your shots.

1–5 Experiment with borders: they can be evenly spaced or uneven. Apply them to portraits, landscapes, and macro shots.

CROSS-PROCESSING

Cross-processing is a popular technique among film photographers. With it, you take a picture using one type of film (usually slide film), and then develop it in chemicals for another type of film (usually color print).

The effects of cross-processing vary depending on the film type used, but you generally get interesting and unexpected changes in color, and high contrast.

With cross-processing apps, you'll get greater color saturation, more contrast, and you can also create vignettes (a darkening around the edges of the frame). If you want to give this a go, some editing apps like CrossProcess, CameraBag, PicSay (Android), Vignette (Android), and Best Camera are well worth trying.

But a word of warning: be aware that cross-processed images are everywhere. Don't overdo it if you want your images to stand out from everyone else's.

The strong colors in this image made it a good subject for editing with a cross-processing app.

This technique works better with some subjects than others. Because of the increase in contrast you get, you may lose detail in parts of the image. Therefore cross-processing works best with simple, straightforward images.

Top Tip
Sometimes portraits can look a little odd, as skin tones change quite a bit through cross-processing. But if you try it with a simple portrait against a plain background, the technique can work really well. Have a go at experimenting with different types of photos to see what works for you.

NO PARKING ANYTIME

Cross-processing apps add character to your images by changing the color and the contrast.

1	3	4		7
2		5	6	

1 The strange effect from cross-processing complements the unusual subject matter of this image. Photo: Emily Portnoi.

2 & 7 Look for subjects with strong or unusual colors, such as this bright metal door and the custom paint job on this car.

3 The cross-processing effect works well with simple images.

4 I knew this background would work well with cross-processing, so I asked the subject to stand in front of it. It always pays to plan ahead.

5 The cross-processing effect suits retro subjects, such as this vintage car. Photo: Jeremy Long.

6 Cross-processing added even more character to this portrait!

TOY
CAMERAS

Some people consider toy cameras to be the most fun you can have with photography, and there are whole cult followings devoted to particular models. A toy camera is lo-fi, cheap, and plastic, and produces imperfect images. However, in the perfect world of digital photography, there's something very appealing about images that have blurry edges, soft focusing, and hit-and-miss exposures.

There are lots of image-editing apps out there with toy camera settings, like PictureShow, Black and White Toy Camera (Android), Plastic Bullet, FX Photo Studio (Windows), CameraBag, Vignette (Android), and Toy Camera.

The two most common toy cameras are the Holga 120 and the Lomo LC-A. The Holga 120 is entirely plastic—even the lens. First produced in the early 1980s for the Chinese mass market, it's cheap and easy to modify. Most important, the images it creates have a look you just can't get from a digital camera.

The Lomo LC-A probably has the biggest cult following among toy camera enthusiasts. It's simple to use and produces high-contrast and high-saturation images, with beautiful vignetting. Lots of Lomo LC-A users like to cross-process (see page 128).

The app used here reproduces the effect of a Lomo camera loaded with cross-processed film.

Toy cameras are probably one of the most popular types of camera that apps emulate. They really can change a mundane photo into something rather special. Different apps do it in different ways, so find the one that works best for you and the way you shoot.

Top Tip
If you're in love with the effects that these apps produce, why not give it a go with a real toy camera and a roll of film? They don't cost that much, and the excitement of picking up your images from the developers is fantastic.

Embrace the imperfect with these apps, which make the lovable qualities of toy cameras possible on your phone.

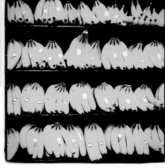

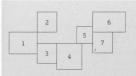

1–7 Apps can mimic the effects of various toy cameras, including the Lomo LC-A (photos 1 and 6), the Holga (photos 2, 4, 5, and 7), and the Diana (photo 3).

FILTERS AND EFFECTS

Most image-editing apps offer filters or effects to apply to your photos. The quality varies, so make sure you only apply these if you need to, and use them only if you're happy with the result.

Filters in the real photography world usually fix onto the end of a lens to give the desired effect. Examples include warming or cooling filters; gradation filters, which darken or lighten areas of your photos; polarizing filters, which reduce reflections or increase definition in clouds and skies; and filters to add vignettes (a darkening of the corners of an image).

All of these filters and many more can be replicated with apps like Pictures Lab (Windows), FX Photo Studio, 101+ PhotoEffects, Cool fx, Photo Stylist (Windows), Vignette (Android), and Perfect Photo.

Filters are often bunched with effects in some apps. Although effects are not based on traditional filters, they're similar to functions you'll find in standard photo-editing software. Effects you'll come across are night vision, sepia, aging, thermal imaging, pencil drawing and sketching, dreamy, watercolor, oil painting, and others.

This shot was taken at sunset. I used a night-vision app to give it this striking effect.

Filters can add subtle changes to your images, like warming or cooling, or they can be very dramatic. Some apps allow you to apply multiple filters to your images, so that you can create and save your own filters and use your favorites again and again. Try to develop a style to your photography and the editing of your shots by using consistent processing techniques. Your photography will be stronger for it in the long run, as you learn what works best for you.

These apps simulate the effects of lens filters, and the results can be as subtle or as striking as you like.

		3	4		6
1					
2			5		

1 A graduation filter was used here to darken the top of the sky, while also fading it out toward the horizon.
2 There's a fine balance between going overboard with an effect and not seeing it enough. This photo with a drawn outline effect gets the balance just right.
3 A vignette effect was added to this shot.
4 A rainbow-colored x-ray effect was added to this portrait . Photo: Emily Portnoi.
5 Sepia toning was used on this photo.
6 This image was achieved by combining sepia toning with a textured effect.

Effects are usually more complicated than filters, as they can add a multitude of variations to your images. You can often combine changes, so for example, you could add a warming effect plus increased saturation and a darkening of the edges.

Top Tip
Don't go overboard with effects; sometimes simple is best. But if the shot really benefits from using one, then go right ahead.

These apps can add a multitude of effects to your images; use them on their own, or combine them as you like.

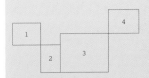

1 Some filter apps can add a cartoon effect to your shots.
2 The app used here gives this photo a hand-drawn look.
3 X-ray apps work well applied to portraits.
4 Many apps can make your photos look like paintings. Try out different artistic styles.

TILT
SHIFT

Take a look at the photos in the gallery on pages 144–145. See how a select area of the image is in focus? This technique is called tilt shift. It's named after a specialized type of camera lens, where if you tilt the lens, you can select specific areas of focus, as well as the position of subjects in the image area. Architectural photographers often use tilt shift to avoid the distorted perspective of buildings in their images.

Where tilt shift really works is in making your images look like they were taken of a miniature world. The selective focus of tilt shift (where the foreground and background is blurred) tricks your mind into thinking that the image is of a tiny scene.

Apps like Instagram, TiltShift Generator, Photo Hub (Windows), Camera 360 (Android), TiltShift, and Tilt Shift Creator (Android) simulate the tilt aspect of these lenses. Select a small part of your image to be sharp, and the rest of the image will be in beautiful soft focus. Selective tilt focusing can look significantly different from using a shallow depth of field, where the plane of focusing goes from the front of the image to the back. With tilt shift, you can have the plane of focus circular, or going from side to side, from any point in the frame you like.

Tilt-shift apps allow you to select a specific area of an image to focus on.

To make your image look like it was taken on one of Gulliver's Travels, start with an image where you're looking down on the subject, so you'll need to find a high vantage point. Images with cars and people as the subject work particularly well.

Some apps allow you to use lineal or a circular/radial blur. Find the main point of interest in your shot—the part you want to draw your viewer's attention to. Then blur around that as much as you need to in order to create an interesting image.

Every image can be a world in miniature if you use the selective focusing of tilt shift apps.

| | | 1 | 3 | | 5 |
| 2 | | | | 4 | |

1 Use tilt-shift apps to make the real world look miniature.
2 Combine an area of focus with dark edges.
3 Use tilt shift to add interest to still-life shots.
4 & 5 Although often used for architectural photography, tilt shift can also be used to produce striking portraits.

1 Applying tilt shift to photos of small objects gives a nice effect.
2 Using tilt shift gives this shot a vintage feel.
3 You don't have to focus on the whole person for a portrait to be effective.
4 Focus on the area that has the most interest.
5 Experiment with tilt shift with all kinds of shots. Photo: Will Scobie.
6 The leading lines formed by the tram cables combine with the focus to make this a successful image.
7 The effect can be more subtle on a tightly cropped image.
8 Try to shoot from a high vantage point.

THROUGH THE VIEWFINDER (TTV)

Through The Viewfinder (TTV or TtV) is an innovative technique that photographers have been using for some time. To do it, you compose an image in the viewfinder of one camera, and take the shot with another.

Usually, the first camera is an old model with a beautiful, bright viewfinder. There may be some interesting guidelines to help frame a subject on the viewfinder, or scratches, unusual textures, or defects in the glass. All this creates an image not just of the subject, but one that's framed by the viewfinder, and the finished image will have signature black edges. The second camera used to capture the shot is normally a digital camera, to allow the photographer to get it just right.

TTV photography can be difficult, as you need the right camera to shoot through, and you also need other equipment to keep light out of the image. But for the phone photographer, it's a whole lot easier. There aren't many apps that do this, but take a look at Lo-Mob and TtV Camera. So get out there, shoot some images, and take a look at the variety of different apps available to make your images look like they've been shot through a beautiful old camera.

This shot was perfectly timed and composed, but the TTV effect gives it a little something extra.

Experiment with different viewfinders in the apps. Some work well, but some have just been added to fill space. Don't go with anything too distracting—this technique should add to the image rather than dominate it.

These apps simulate the effects of TTV photography, where two cameras—one with a vintage viewfinder, the other usually digital —create a unique effect.

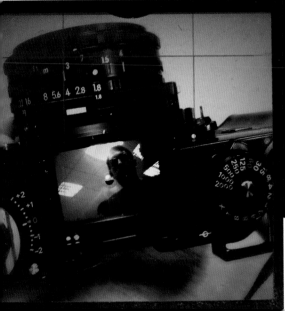

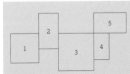

	2			5	
1				4	
		3			

1, 2 & 4 TTV is most effective when applied to uncluttered images. Keep your composition simple and avoid having too many distractions in the shot.
3 A TTV setup.
5 The choice of subject and the use of black and white combine well with the TTV effect in this image.

BORDERS, FRAMES, AND OBJECTS

The options for adding borders, frames, or objects with apps are almost limitless. There are so many apps out there—like Photo Finish, Photo Hub (Windows), Joy Camera, PicSay (Android), and Iron Camera—that can help with this technique. Each one has different things to add to your image.

Borders are almost self-explanatory. You may want to add a uniform white border around your image, or you may just want a round border; most possibilities are covered with these apps.

When it comes to frames, the choices are endless. Add a gold frame to turn your image into a gallery masterpiece; make your photo look like a postage stamp; or create the effect of shooting on film, with all the details that go with it. All sorts of fuzzy and textured edges are available. If you can think of it, chances are someone else has too, and they've made an app for it.

As for what kind of objects you can add to your image, the list is endless. Some examples are speech bubbles, silly moustaches, hats, glasses, stars, hearts, and different background scenes. Some look good, some OK, and some look terrible.

These apps can be used to add bold effects to everyday scenes.

Don't go overboard with borders, frames, or objects, as they can look tacky and gimmicky. Your image may look fine on your phone, but as soon as you upload it to a website it may not look so great. You want people to see the image itself, not the border, frame, or object you've added.

Take care when applying these apps, and ask yourself: Does the image really need it? If the answer is yes, apply away; if the answer is no, walk away.

These apps are all about adding interest with borders, frames, or other objects.

I want beer!

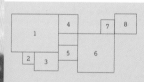

		4		7	8
1					
2	3	5	6		

1 & 4 Simple borders are often the most effective as do will not distract from your subject.

2 & 7 These sketchy borders enhance the mood of these shots. Photo: Kevin Birk.

3 A bolder choice of border can work well, but it's best to apply it to a simpler image.

5, 6 & 8 Plan ahead and ask your subject to adopt suitable poses to help you place your objects in the shot to maximum effect.

USING
THE
SHOT

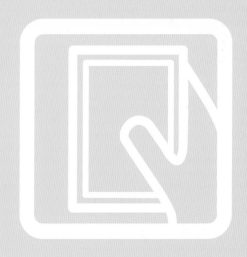

BEST PRACTICE: BACKING UP AND SAVING YOUR IMAGES

It's worth taking time to look at a few best-practice tips that can help you get the most from your phone photography.

In terms of saving your images, most apps do this automatically. No problem, you might think. But you should check how they save your images. It's really important that you set your apps to save at the highest resolution (or the biggest size) possible.

Why? Well, you may not only view your images on your phone. A low-resolution image can look great on your phone, but when you upload it to a website or computer, and view it on a bigger screen, you'll notice a huge difference in quality. The same applies if you want to print an image out: too low a resolution, and you'll end up with a poor-quality result.

Always save your images at the biggest size possible. This will depend on your phone, of course, as each model's resolution is different. But if you save your images at the largest size, you shouldn't lose any image quality.

Backing up your images is just essential. We all know that technology can go wrong, and in the same way you back up information on your computer, you really should back up the images on your phone. You only need to lose important information or photos once to learn the hard way. Don't put yourself through that pain, and back up. Download your images to your computer, copy them to CD, save them on Flickr—just make sure they're not in one place only.

There are various apps that can really help with Wi-Fi/Bluetooth file transfers—check out Photo Transfer and Bluetooth File Transfer (Android).

For a really advanced, cool way of backing up, take a look at the wonderful SugarSync (various platforms). This program saves your images online, and has an automatic sync function, so you never need to worry about backing up again. This is just one of many similar products out there, so check them out.

UPLOADING TO MULTIPLE SITES

So you took some great photos, using all your creativity, and got some fantastic results from exploring apps and all they have to offer. Why not share them with friends, family, colleagues, or even the whole Internet?

Some people set up a dedicated website, blog, or social network account for their phone images. Most people, though, just want to share them in a few select places online.

The really great thing about apps like Instagram, Vignette (Android), and Best Camera is that they have the built-in option to upload to several different places at once, such as Facebook, Twitter, or Flickr. With one tap, you can have your images just where you want them.

If you want to upload your images to sites that aren't associated with a particular app, take a look at some of the following, which allow you to access as many sites as you like. Start by looking at Pixelpipe, PhotoScatter, and PicPiz (Android). Pixelpipe is also available in an Android version.

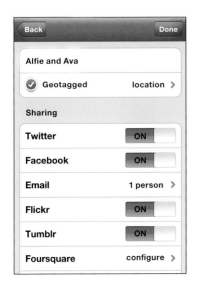

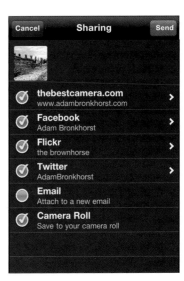

FLICKR

Flickr is an online video- and photo-hosting site. That's the official description, but actually, it's much more than that. Sure, you can post your photos, and store them all in one place (great as an online backup; see page 159). But really, that's the tip of the iceberg. Flickr is a fantastic way to connect with other photographers and find like-minded people.

You can comment on other people's photos, and receive comments and advice on yours; it's an amazing source of inspiration. Just looking at other people's images can really help you develop in your photography.

The discussion forums and groups are a brilliant way to gain knowledge about most subjects: there are groups dedicated to almost any kind of camera or genre. Groups can be geographical as well, so you can meet up with other local photographers.

Lots of apps help you access and upload your images to Flickr, but start with Flicka (Android), Flickr, Darkslide, Flickr Droid (Android), and Flickr for Windows 7.

Don't think that Flickr is just for photographers with "proper" cameras, or that phone photography won't be welcome. Flickr tracks lots of stats, and you may be surprised to learn that the most popular camera for images taken on Flickr is actually the iPhone.

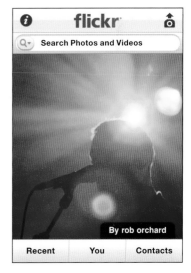

SOCIAL NETWORKS

Most people are now very familiar with social networks, which are websites that help you to connect with like-minded people. Here, you'll find a few of the most popular ones, and the apps that help you access them more easily with your phone.

Twitter
www.twitter.com
Twitter is a microblogging site, where users can share small bits of information via "tweets" up to 140 characters long. Tweets are often posted with images. Due to the immediacy of Twitter, and the shortness of the messages, users often post multiple tweets a day. In this way, they differ from blogs, where you usually only post one blog entry per day, or even per week. There are several apps you can use to access Twitter, and Twitter itself has a very usable app.

Tumblr
www.tumblr.com
Tumblr makes blogging text, photos, quotes, links, music, and videos incredibly simple. It's fully customizable, so you can totally change the look and feel of your blog to how you want it to be. Lots of people use Tumblr as a very quick and easy way to blog their phone images. The official Tumblr App is called Tumblerette.

Instagram
instagr.am
Instagram may not be a traditional social network, but it's worth mentioning here, as it works so well as one. It's a very simple app where you can shoot an image, edit it with photo filters, and upload your image to Instagram's own photo-sharing section (see also page 170).

Flickr

www.flickr.com

Flickr is probably the best online photo
management and sharing application. It's
so popular with photographers that it's now
hosting over five billion images. Flickr has
its own app, and there are several other apps
that allow you to access the site (see page
162 for more).

Facebook

www.facebook.com

The biggest social network site out there.
Lots of photographers use Facebook to
upload their images, share them with
friends, or create and manage a page for
their photography or photography business.
There are numerous apps out there that
allow you to access Facebook.

GEOTAGGING

Have you ever seen a photo online, and wondered where it was taken? Geotagging can show you the exact location where an image was shot, and it can pinpoint that location on a map.

Geotagging works by adding geographical information, like latitude and longitude coordinates, to images. Many phones now have a very accurate built-in Global Positioning System (GPS) that makes this possible. Geotagging can be used for recording where you shot something, or you can use it to research new locations to shoot in.

Apps that can help with geotagging include Photo Geo and Geotagger (Android). There are some shooting apps that automatically geotag your images, although you may have to switch this function on if you want to use it.

Other apps can highlight fantastic locations for photography, where you simply click on a map and see what other people have already shot. Take a look at AroundShare, Photo Location (Windows), and Panoramio (Windows).

With Clixtr, you can shoot a photo, upload it to the app's website, and if you're near a spot where lots of other people are uploading media, (like a concert or major event), Clixtr will use the GPS signal to group all of the images into an album.

TAGGING

Tagging is a way of adding descriptive information to digital images. This information is also known as metadata, and helps you or anyone else to find your image when searching online or on a computer.

For example, let's say you've taken a picture of your friend on a bench in the park. You may want to add tags such as: park, Alfie, bench, New York, USA, America, summer, clouds, sky, grass, outdoors, trees, friend, iPhone, etc. That way, if you want to search online or in your photo library for any images of Alfie in New York, you'll be able to find that one quickly, along with any other shots with those tags.

You can also tag your friends and contacts in photos, so when you upload images to, say, Facebook, they'll be notified.

Apps such as Instagram and Facebook App (Windows) allow you to tag images. There are also some apps dedicated to tagging, like 10X Camera Tools Pro, Viewdle SocialCamera (Android), and Phototagger.

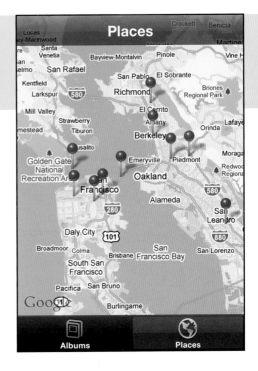

APPS THAT DO IT ALL

This book focuses on the different processes you use in phone photography: shooting, editing, and using the shot, and how you can find different apps to enhance each of these.

But rather than use a specific app to shoot an image, another to edit and save it, then a third to upload your image to various websites, you could choose one of the apps that helpfully roll all these processes into one. They can make life a whole lot easier, as you don't have to keep jumping from one app to another.

The downside of these apps is that you'll lose some control: for example, when shooting, there are apps to help with image composition, (page 22), getting your shot level (page 38), and setting the focus and exposure (page 26). When editing, specific apps give you more creative options: changing the saturation of individual colors or converting to black-and-white, for example (page 108).

With all-in-one apps, you may also be limited to which websites you can upload your images to.

That said, combined apps can be really handy to have, and some of the best are outlined on the following pages.

Instagram

Instagram is rapidly growing in popularity. This app works so well, and is so easy to use, that the word "Instagrammable" was coined by the *New York Times*. Instagram photos have appeared on the front page of the *Wall Street Journal*.

With it, you can shoot an image, then almost instantly apply any of the filters or effects that the app offers. Once you're happy with your edit, you can add a geographical location to the image (see page 166), and upload it to a few different social networks (see page 164).

The image also gets uploaded to Instagram's own gallery and social network.

It's a very clever app that syncs with your phone contacts and Facebook and Twitter accounts, and will show you which of your friends is also using Instagram. It's an almost perfect app. Start using it today if you can.

Vignette

If you're an Android phone user, you need Vignette in your life. This is the best Android app for shooting, editing, and sharing. Vignette has an amazing array of filters, effects, and frames. When you're ready, you can upload preview-quality photos. They aren't currently full-size images, but at least you can upload these to various social media sites.

Camera Genius

Billed as "the camera app you wished your iPhone shipped with," this app does seem to have it all. It's a great shooting app with multiple options: touch anywhere onscreen to fire the shutter; use grids, burst mode, timers, or anti-shake; and set the focus and exposure separately.

You can also edit and crop your shot using a whole host of filters and effects, and add borders. Once you've done all that, you can share your image by uploading it to lots of different sites. If that's not enough, it also includes a photography manual with tips and tricks on a variety of subjects.

Best Camera

This app was created by a professional photographer whose philosophy was "the best camera is the one that's with you." He got tired of using five or six apps to shoot, edit, and share. So he created this app to do it all in one place. There's a great community of Best Camera users, where people share their images and the filters they used to create them.

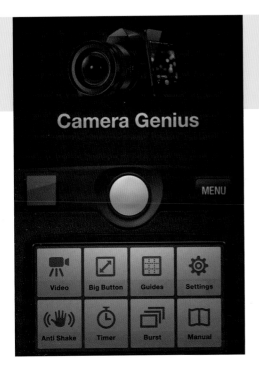

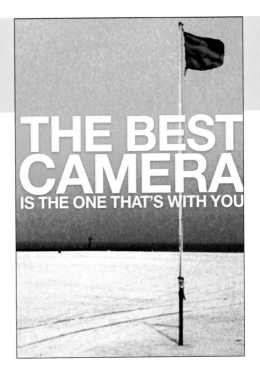

TAKING IT FARTHER

GALLERY SLIDE SHOW

If you want to show your phone images to other people, there are two options: use your phone's camera gallery, or try a dedicated app. It'll display your images automatically in a beautiful slide show.

Your phone's built-in options may allow you to display photos randomly, or to select image transitions (how the picture swipes across the screen, or fades in and out).

The advantage of using a dedicated app is that you'll have far more control over your slide show. So if you're not happy with the transitions your phone supplies, a dedicated app will usually have many more to choose from.

An app may also give you the option of having background music. You can choose from tunes that the app supplies, or you can sometimes pick a track from your own music library.

Take a look at apps like Photo Slide (Android), Animoto, Photo Show, Gallery (Android), SlideShowPro, SlideShow (Windows), or Photo Show (Windows).

Slide show apps give you creative control when making photo presentations, right down to the choice of music.

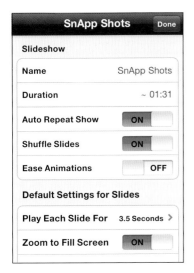

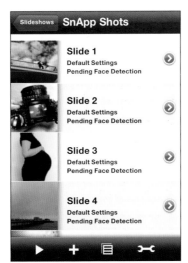

LIGHT
METERS

Professional photographers rely on lots of specialized equipment to help them achieve the image they want.

The amount of light a camera captures dramatically affects the look and feel of a photo. When it comes to this, there's no better piece of equipment for the professional than a light meter (also known as an exposure meter). It makes a calculation based on the amount of light in a given shot, which tells the photographer how long to expose the shot for.

Although they probably won't be as accurate as a professional light meter, you'll be surprised by the level of sophistication you can get from apps such as LightMeter, PhotoCalc, The Pocket Light Meter, Light Meter Gadget (Android), and Tiny Light Meter (Android).

Try using them with your phone photography, but if you're shooting with an old film camera and you don't know if there'll be enough light to take a photo, you can use one of these apps to check. Remember, they won't be 100 percent accurate, but they should be able to put you in the right ballpark.

Flash Exposure

⚠ There is enough light in the scene and the image will be properly exposed.

🔳 **Guide Number**	100	›
🔳 **Aperture**	f/11	›
🔳 **ISO**	100	›
🔳 **Flash Power**	Full	›
🔳 **Subject Distance**	9' 11"	

Touch the calculator next to the component you would like calculated based upon the other values.

Depth | Flash | Sunrise | Reference | More

Solar Calculator

Date	17 May 2011	›
Location	New York	›

Twilight Begins	10:13
Sunrise	10:39
Solar Noon	17:53
Sunset	01:00
Twilight Ends	01:34

Depth | Flash | Sunrise | Reference | More

DEPTH-OF-FIELD CALCULATORS

Depth of field is the distance between the nearest and farthest objects that appear in focus in a photograph. So an image where the background is blurred, but the foreground is in focus, is described as having a shallow depth of field. A landscape shot, for example, where everything is in focus, has a large depth of field.

Various apps such as PHOforPHO (Android), DOF Calculator (Android), PhotoCalc, and DOF Depth of Field Calculator (Windows) can help you calculate the depth of field for your shots based on the focal length of the lens, the aperture you're shooting at, and your subject's distance.

Some of these apps make calculations based on data that you've inputted. Others are very clever and can calculate the settings automatically. You can even get apps that show you real-time settings; you can adjust those settings for the result you want.

Some depth-of-field apps, as well as the light meter apps on page 178, can calculate the flash power you need to get a correct exposure. There are quite a few apps that cover both depth of field and exposure.

Depth of Field

Focal Length	50mm >
Aperture	f/11 >
Subject Distance	10' >

Near Limit	7' 12"
Far Limit	13' 5"
Total Depth	5' 5"
Hyperfocal Dist.	39' 3"

Depth   Flash   Sunrise   Reference   More

LEARNING APPS

Many learning apps focus on the technical side of photography and can help you understand your camera, photography terms, and specific techniques. They can include advice from professionals, and show you how to set up your camera to achieve a certain look.

One of the biggest is Nikon's Learn & Explore. It features some great articles by very talented photographers, with photos and videos as support. Lessons are pitched at beginner, intermediate, or advanced level.

Android shooters should look at Photography Trainer, which has step-by-step instructions and dozens of sample photos, along with tutorials and tips. Another neat app is Pro Photographer Prep Quiz.

This is based on the Certified Professional Photographers (CPP) exam, and it can help you learn over 200 terms and concepts with multiple-choice questions, flashcards, and so on.

Learn Digital Photography is another great app where you can receive a tip of the week and participate in contests. It has digital camera reviews, explains techniques, and more.

"How to make good photos with a reflex camera for Windows Phone 7" may not be the catchiest name for an app, but it does cover tips and tricks from the professionals, themes, composition, and colors. If you're a Windows phone user, you should also look at PhotoWiz for helpful advice on how to raise your photography game.

Image editing is a whole field of knowledge in itself, and some big-name photographers employ people just to handle this stage—that's how complicated a task it can be. But don't fret, as there are a few apps out there that can give you the fundamentals of image editing.

Start by looking at Understanding Photoshop—Quick Fixes. This app has a range of ways to help you learn this complex software, from training videos to hands-on files that you download to your computer, as well as interactive quizzes and a quick reference guide.

The Learn Photoshop App for Android is a book-based app, but it has lots of information and can take you through simple techniques, like cropping your images, and more advanced editing methods, such as color correction.

Photography theory is probably the smallest category of learning apps, as they can be quite specialized. They probably don't appeal to the average shooter who just wants to know how to take a good photo.

Unique apps like PICBOD (Picturing The Body) fall into this market. This is an undergraduate class run at Coventry University in the UK. They've taken the big step of putting parts of this university degree into an app, for anyone to download and get a taste of undergraduate-level photography. So if you're interested in "learning how to address complex aesthetic, creative, and technical issues, along with the visual messages associated with the photographic encounter with the body," then this app is for you.

MODEL RELEASE FORMS

Let's say you've taken a fantastic shot on a phone or DSLR camera. If you think it's good enough to use in an advert, sell a print of it, or use it in any commercial capacity, then legally you should get permission from anyone who appears in the image to use their likeness. The best way to do this is to ask your subjects to sign something called a model release form.

There are many standard forms available online that you can print off and get people to sign. Or you could use one of the dedicated apps such as Easy Release, iD Release, Easy Release (Android), and Model Release Pal (Android), where your subject can fill in all their contact details, date of birth etc., and sign the form on your phone's screen.

These make the whole process much more straightforward, as you're always carrying the forms with you. Once signed, you can email the forms to yourself and the subject. It's as easy as that. Be aware that if you're taking shots of children, you'll need a parent or guardian to sign the form on their behalf.

When these app model release forms first came out, some people thought that they wouldn't hold up as legal documents. But you'll be pleased to know that some major image libraries are now accepting them. So if they're happy with them, you should be too.

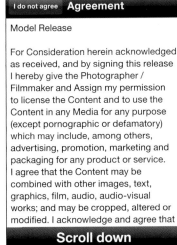

LOCATION FINDERS

These days, most phones have a Global Positioning System (GPS) built into them. What this means is that they're capable of recording exactly where an image was taken, or showing you where someone else has taken an image.

Apps such as The Photographer's Ephemeris and Foto Brisko highlight specific places on a map, and show you images that were taken around that area. This is very useful if you're looking for a location to shoot in, or if you're visiting somewhere and want to get some inspiration for your photography.

Location Recorder (Android) and PHOforPHO (Android) can help you record your precise location, so if you're shooting with a DSLR and want to remember or geotag (see page 166) where you took a shot, these apps will help.

MagicHour, Golden Hour Photos (Android), and The Photographer's Ephemeris help you calculate sunrise or sunset times for locations, so you can work out the perfect time to shoot and capture that great golden light. They can even tell you when the sun will be in the perfect position to avoid shadows.

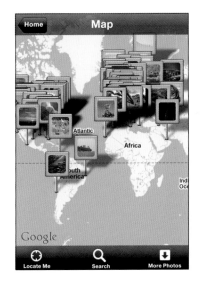  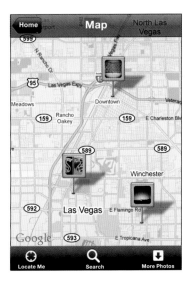

LIGHTING DIAGRAMS

If you use studio lighting for your shots, or you're planning a shoot with any kind of lighting and you want to show someone else your setup, then apps like Strobox, Sylights, and Lighting Studio (Android) are for you, and could make life much easier.

Let's say you've been planning where you want to position studio lights at a shoot. You could either spend the first 30 minutes telling your assistants where you want them, or you could show them a beautiful electronic diagram of your lighting setup. Even better, you could e-mail them your diagram in advance, straight from the app, so the lights are all ready for you when you arrive.

I often shoot company profile shots for corporate clients, and I find it very handy to use a lighting diagram app to document the shoot setup after it's taken place. That way, when I'm asked at a later date to do more profile shots, I've kept a really accurate record of everything. It's easy then to match new shots to the previous ones.

Send E-mail

Save to Photo Album

Cancel

OTHER APPS TO TAKE IT FARTHER

There's a huge variety of apps out there that can help you with your photography, whether you're shooting with your phone or an expensive DSLR, whether you're a professional photographer or just someone who likes snapping away.

There are quite a few apps, like DSLR Camera Remote, Camera Remote (Android), and DSLR Camera Remote Professional (Android), that allow you to use your phone to control the settings and fire your DSLR camera. This could come in very handy on shoots if you want to get an unusual camera angle, or if it's difficult to fire the camera manually.

The wonderful PhotoAssist is almost invaluable for anyone planning a photo or video shoot with lots of gear. The app allows you to create and track equipment lists for various types of shoots, so you always have what you need at the start, and you never leave any of it behind when it's over.

Along the same lines is the app Second Shootr. This is handy if you're shooting a wedding and you want to make sure you have all the details you need, like venue address, ceremony times, best man's name, lists of group shots, etc.

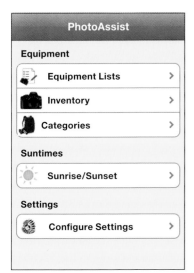

PhotoAssist

Equipment

📋 Equipment Lists >

📷 Inventory >

🎒 Categories >

Suntimes

☀️ Sunrise/Sunset >

Settings

⚙️ Configure Settings >

Sun & Moon **Location** **Map**

Latitude (N)　　Longitude (E)　　Tracking
✛　+50.8418　　-0.2706　　**OFF**

Date/Time　　　　　　　　　　Tracking
🕐　10 Oct 2011 15:45　　**OFF**

Sat 8 Oct	14	15
Sun 9 Oct	15	30
Mon 10 Oct	16	45
Tues 11 Oct	17	00
Wed 12 Oct	18	15

🌙　　🌀　　▶　　✳　　●●●
Sun & Moon　Exposure　DoF　Diffraction　More

← 　☀️ ☀️ ☀️　 **Edit**

🎞️ **FP4+**
　35mm, ISO 125

🥤 **R09 (1+40)**　　　　　　　>
　500 ml = 12 + 488 ml

🌡️ **12:00 min at 20°C**

📄

Development:　**12:00**　▭▭▭▭
Stop Bath:　**1:00**　▭▭▭▭
Fixing:　**5:00**　▭▭▭▭
Hypo Clear:　**2:00**　▭▭▭▭
Rinsing:　**10:30**　▭▭▭▭

00:00.0

Start　　　**Reset**

The PhotoBuddy app has an amazing array of features. Among many other things, it can calculate sunrise or sunset times or the moon phase for a given date; it helps you measure distances with the built-in camera; and it has built-in exposure presets and allows you to calculate exposure changes. It has depth-of-field guides, and it sets the white balance of your camera (the balance of red, green, and blue needed to produce a normal-looking white) with a list of color temperatures for common light situations.

If you're into shooting and developing your own films at home, you need an app called Massive Dev Chart (various platforms) in your life. This amazing app can tell you the exact development times needed for most films on the market. It's fully user-configurable, so you can input the type of film, chemicals, and so on, to get the perfect development times.

One of the best features is that it also has a built-in multi-step timer for all of the processes (developing, stopping, fixing, and final rinse) that you need to work through.

There really is an app for everything. Just go out there and find the one that helps you do what you want to do.

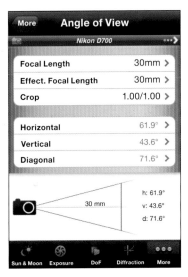

ACCESSORIES

MACRO LENSES

Accessories and lenses can help you to be just as creative with your photography as a great app can.

Macro (close-up) photography is covered in more detail on page 50. However, it's possible to buy a dedicated lens that attaches to your phone and allows you to shoot and focus a lot closer than usual.

How close? These lenses can let you focus between 10–23mm from your subject. You'll soon be seeing the world in super miniature, and it's very easy to become obsessed with macro photography.

There are quite a few add-on lenses available. Some of them are phone and model specific, while some of them are universal. Take a look around and see what you can find; generally, they're a worthwhile purchase. Some macro lenses can really zoom in on a subject, so be aware that this may be too close for you. If you want to show the world off in minute detail, however, they're perfect.

A macro lens attachment will improve your camera's ability to focus. Photo on top right: Kevin Lawrence. Photo on bottom left: Sarah Lawrence.

When shooting with a macro lens, it can help to use a tripod to steady your phone. Because you're shooting so close to your subject, you may find that any slight movement will affect where your area of focus is, so a tripod will help you achieve perfect framing and exposure.

As you're holding your camera right over the subject, you may also be stopping light from reaching it. So think about where the light's coming from, how it's falling, and how you can position your phone where you want it to be.

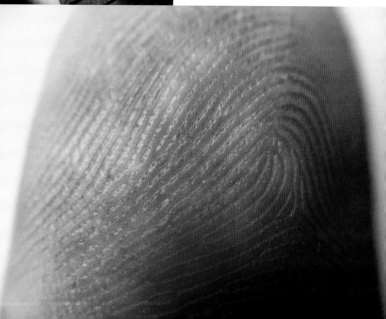

Macro lenses can add a whole new dimension to your photography, allowing you to see the world in super close-up.

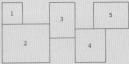

1		3		5
	2		4	

1–5 Experiment by photographing everyday items. Getting in close with a macro lens can create some unusual images.

TELEPHOTO LENSES

Your camera will come with a standard-focal-length lens (see page 14). This is a good all-around lens, but what happens if you want to get closer to your subject? You could change position and move yourself right up close, but it may not be that easy.

The alternative is to get hold of a telephoto (long focal length) lens. They look a little weird attached to your phone, but they need to be pretty big to bring your subject closer to you. Some lenses attach directly to your phone and some sit in a case that fits around it.

Telephoto lenses can increase your camera's focal length by up to eight times. Play around with the type of shots that you can get with them: use them at concerts, on buildings, zoom right in on your subject, or pick out details in landscapes.

Add a telephoto lens to your phone and you'll be able to shoot faraway subjects.

Top Tip
With a telephoto lens, your images will be less stable than when you're using a standard lens. You're zoomed in on a shot, so any slight movement will be exaggerated. You can avoid this by using a tripod (see page 212) to keep things shake-free.

Telephoto lenses increase the focal length of your phone's lens, and really allow you to zoom in on your subject.

1–2 & 4–5 These two scenes were shot with normal lenses and telephoto lenses. You can get in so much closer with a telephoto lens. **3** A telephoto lens attachment.

WIDE-ANGLE FISH-EYE LENSES

The magnification and field of view that a lens provides is defined by its focal length. Many phone cameras have a focal length of around 30mm. This means the lens is wide enough to shoot landscapes, but can still handle portraits without distorting people's features too much.

If you want to shoot a scene that's wider than your lens will allow, it's possible to buy tiny wide-angle lenses for your phone's camera. Some are plastic and some are glass. With glass, you'll tend to lose less quality in your pictures than you would with a plastic lens.

There are different ways of attaching the lenses. Some models use a detachable magnetic ring. Some come with a sticky, jelly-like attachment while on others, the lenses form part of a case that fits around the phone.

Some wide-angle lenses give you a 0.68× wider shot than the standard lens on your phone. This type of lens is particularly useful for capturing landscapes, large crowds, and concerts, as well as unusual portraits.

There are also a few fish-eye (extremely wide) lenses available that can give your images a full 180-degree field of view.

Use a fish-eye lens to produce quirky portraits.

Both wide-angle and fish-eye lenses will distort perspective to a certain extent, so be aware of that when shooting, or make the most of this feature.

With wide-angle lenses, fill your frame to capture as much detail as possible. Crowd shots work really well. When using fish-eye lenses, try and capture some crazy portraits, get right up close, and have fun with the distortion and false perspective.

Fish-eye and wide-angle lenses allow you to shoot much wider than you usually would with your phone.

	2		6
1			5
	3	4	

1 & 6 A wide-angle lens is a good accessory to have when you're photographing a crowd.
2, 3 & 5 Get up close to your subject with the lens for dramatic results.
4 Play around with distorted perspective when shooting landscapes.

FILTERS

Filters for SLR cameras are fairly standard accessories, but it's also possible to buy them for phone cameras.

Using filters, you can achieve starburst, polarized, heart frame, panoramic, and kaleidoscope effects, among many others. Take a look at the gallery on pages 210–211 to see some examples.

Filters can attach to your phone with a reusable adhesive ring that leaves no residue on your phone. If it loses its stickiness, you can gently clean the ring with soapy water to refresh it. Filters offer fantastic value for the money (they're usually made of plastic or acrylic, rather than glass) and they're well worth buying, even as a first purchase, to see if you like these kinds of "add-on" lenses. And, of course, you can have great fun experimenting with them.

This image was taken using a kaleidoscope filter.

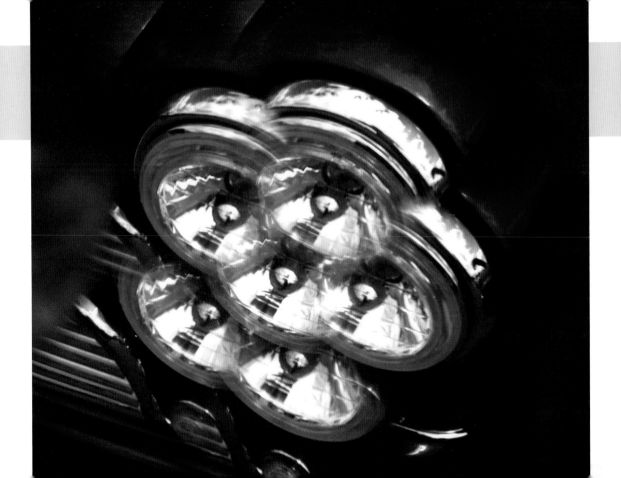

If the filter loses its stickiness, you may need to hold it over the phone. As with all these accessories, make sure it lines up perfectly over the lens. Otherwise, you'll end up blocking out some of the image and shooting the edge of the filter rather than your subject.

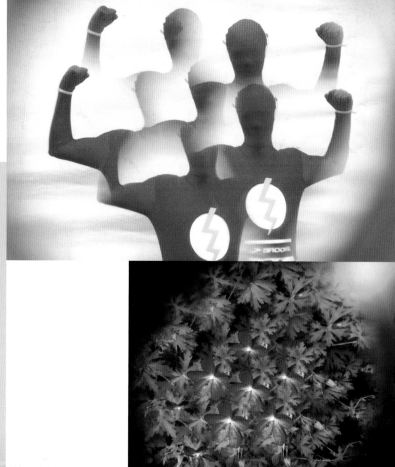

Filters are a fun and low-cost way of enhancing your photography with different patterns, shapes, and effects.

| 1 | | 3 | | | 6 |
| 2 | | 4 | 5 | | |

1, 2 & 6 These effects were achieved using a kaleidoscope filter attachment.
3–5 A starburst filter was used to blur the edges of these photos.

TRIPODS

If you're doing any kind of photography where you need to keep your camera steady, then a tripod's what you need. It can be one of a photographer's most useful pieces of kit.

How does this translate to phone photography? If you want to take a self-portrait, a group shot with you in it, a night-time shot, a long exposure, shoot a movie, or even just watch a film on your phone, then a tripod is just the tool for the job.

There are so many types of tripods out there. Some are specifically made for phones. Some clamp onto your phone while others slide into a special holder. Lots of these holders have the universal tripod mount built into them. This is great, as it allows you to fix your phone onto almost any tripod. So if you have an old model for your "proper" camera lying around, you can use it with your phone.

Top Tip

Some tripod mounts are really lightweight, so although they're stable, they may not be that strong. Take care with your phone, and never totally trust your mount, just in case your phone makes a break for the concrete floor. It has been known to happen.

A tripod can be invaluable when shooting in low light, with a telephoto lens, or in any scenario where you need to keep your camera steady.

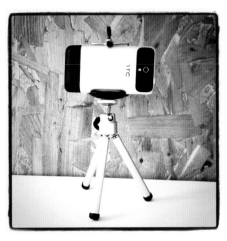

OTHER ACCESSORIES

There's a whole world of useful phone accessories out there. Check out the wonderful photojojo.com for more ideas, and also look on Internet auction sites.

Cases

So many types of cases are available: there are ones made of hard plastic, soft plastic, rubber, or even metal. All protect your phone, and some of them even add functionality, like built-in lenses or the option of adding a camera strap.

Covers

Here we're talking about stick-on covers that attach to the back of your phone. They don't offer that much protection, nor do they improve your photography, but they can be great fun. You can get really cool covers that imitate classic Polaroid, Leica, or Lomo cameras, for example.

Underwater Gear

Yes, you can shoot while scuba diving! There are great waterproof cases that you can take to the beach or use on the slopes—anywhere your phone may get wet. It's even possible to buy underwater headphones. Just be aware that cases may leak if the seals aren't perfect. It's always best to spend the most you can; don't buy a cheap case. If you put your phone underwater, even in one of the better cases, you're always taking a risk.

iPhone SLR Mount

Believe it or not, you can now get an accessory that allows you to mount any Canon or Nikon SLR lens to an iPhone. A crazy idea, but one that has the potential to produce some very creative results. The accessory comes with a special case that fits onto the iPhone and an adapter to mount your SLR lens. You are best using an old film SLR lens though, as it seems that in mounting a lens to your iPhone, you lose around two stops of exposure. So an old lens that has an aperture ring where you can manually change your aperture will give you the best results, as modern digital SLR lenses don't have this facility. You will also need to manually focus your lens to get a sharp image because tapping on the screen in the normal way will not change the focus of your lens.

The possibilities really are endless with this accessory—mount a wide-angle lens, a telephoto lens, or even a prime lens. You can also get Holga and Diana lens adapters for digital SLR cameras so there is no reason why you can't mount one of these on your iPhone now.

Grips

Grips can help you create videos with less shake. The phone slips into a case with supports for you to hold, so you can keep movement smooth and stable when shooting. Some grips even have a cold shoe adapter that can house a light or microphone.

Battery Packs

One downside of phone photography is that it tends to drain your battery. There are various power-saving tricks, like switching off your phone's Bluetooth or Wi-Fi, and reducing your screen's brightness. But if you really want to avoid running out of juice, take a look at battery packs. You charge the pack up, and if your phone battery's running low, you can attach it for an extra power boost.

GLOSSARY

35mm film
A commonly used film type that gives a rectangular-shaped image.

120 film
A film type that gives square-shaped images with lots of detail. 120 is also known as medium format.

Color saturation
An expression for the purity of a color.

Contrast
The overall difference in brightness between the light areas and the dark areas in a photograph. If the difference is large, the image has a high contrast. If the difference is small, the image has a low contrast.

Cross-processing
A technique used in film photography where a photo is taken using a particular type of film and is then developed using chemicals for another film type. This creates interesting color changes. The effect can be replicated by some apps.

Depth of field
The area of sharp focus within an image.

Digital noise
Similar to grain in film photography, digital noise occurs when shooting in low light and appears on the photograph as a loss of definition.

Digital single-lens reflex camera (DSLR)
A camera where the viewfinder image is seen through the same lens that is used to take the photograph. This is made possible by a series of mirrors called a pentaprism, which present a corrected scene to the viewfinder. DSLRs are the preferred choice of professional photographers.

Exposure
The amount of light that falls onto the sensor. If there is too much light, the photo will be too bright and overexposed. If there is too little light, the photo will be too dark and underexposed.

Exposure meters
See *Light meters*.

Filters
Attachments that can produce varied effects on images, such as making photos warmer, cooler, or adding colors. The effect of a physical filter can be replicated by some apps.

Fish-eye lens
A wide-angle lens that produces a distorted view of a scene.

High Dynamic Range (HDR)
Uses image-processing software to combine different exposures of the same scene. The resulting photograph shows a greater tonal range between light and dark areas.

Infrared film
Captures light wavelengths that are outside the spectrum of the human eye to create unusual photos.

Instant film
Film type, such as Polaroid, that produces an "instant" printed photograph. Several apps can recreate this look, including adding a characteristic white border around the image.

Interval shooting
Photographing a fast-moving subject by taking a quick burst of images.

Light meters
Gadgets or apps that tell the photographer how long to expose a shot for based on calculations of the amount of light. They are also known as exposure meters.

Macro photography
Close-up photography of small objects. Macro lens adapters are available as accessories for smartphones.

Medium format
See *120 film*.

Multiple exposure
The technique of overlaying two or more shots to create a new, multi-layered photograph.

Rule of thirds
A composition technique that uses imaginary lines to split the frame into thirds horizontally and vertically. Subjects can then be positioned at the points where the lines cross to produce a balanced composition. Some apps can overlay an actual grid onto the phone's screen to aid with composition.

Self-timer
The camera is set up to shoot and the shutter set to fire after a short delay.

Sensor
The light-sensitive chip that captures the image.

Shutter
The mechanism in a cameras used to determine when the sensor is exposed to light. Unlike a camera, there is no physical shutter in a phone.

Shutter lag
The slight delay between pressing the shutter button and the camera taking the photograph.

Shutter speed
The length of time that the sensor is exposed to light.

Slide film
A type of film that produces positive rather than negative strips of images.

Telephoto lens
A long focal length lens that allows the photographer to zoom in on a distant subject.

Through the viewfinder (TTV)
A technique where an image is composed through the viewfinder of one camera but the shot is taken with another camera.

Tilt shift
A specialized lens that is tilted to select specific areas of focus. These lenses are used in architectural photography to avoid distorted perspective, but they can also be used creatively to make scenes look like miniatures.

Time-lapse photography
A series of photographs of a subject taken at regular periods of time.

Toy cameras
Simple, cheap, plastic cameras that produce imperfect, yet appealing, images.

Vignette
A darkening around the edge of a photograph's frame.

Wide-angle lenses
Lenses that capture a wider area of a scene.

RESOURCES

The smartphone marketplace and apps by their very nature are forever evolving. What is fresh and current one month may seem dated and stale the next. One of the best ways to find out about new apps is to look on the web. Here is a list of some great sites that give lots and lots of information about the latest apps, developments in technology, and what's hot.

Android Market
Online store for Android apps.
market.android.com

Android Tapp
Android app blog, featuring news, reviews, and interviews with app developers.
www.androidtapp.com

App Brain
Marketplace for Android apps.
www.appbrain.com

Best Android Apps Review
Reviews of Android apps, plus tutorials.
www.bestandroidappsreview.com

Best App Site
Reviews of the latest apps for the iPhone, iPad, and iPod Touch.
www.bestappsite.com

Coolsmartphone
Reviews of Windows, Android, and iPhone.
www.coolsmartphone.com

Gizmodo
Gadget and technology blog.
gizmodo.com

Into Mobile
News and reviews for Android, Windows, Apple, and Blackberry.
www.intomobile.com

iPhoneography
Blog dedicated to iPhone photography and technology.
www.iphoneography.com

Mac App Store
Official Apple site for downloading apps.
www.apple.com/mac/app-store/

Techradar
Technology news and reviews.
www.techradar.com

Windows Phone
Marketplace for Windows apps.
marketplace.windowsphone.com

INDEX

ACKNOWLEDGMENTS

I'd like to thank everyone who has let me take their photo for this book, it's been great fun shooting the images. HTC and Nokia for lending me some phones. The fantastic PhotoJoJo.com for sending me a bundle of very cool accessories and for supporting phone photography so well.

All the people that have helped out with the publishing of this book, especially Jane, Isheeta, and Rachel (without whom my words wouldn't be so succinct).

Also to Donna Spencer www.flickr.com/photos/lomod, Rob Orchard www.flickr.com/photos/rob_orchard, Simon Pollock www.gtvone.com

My friends and family for putting up with me taking their photos all the time and for always being there for me. And last but not least, my son, daughter, and wonderful wife. Everything I do, I do it for you…..to quote Bryan Adams.